DATE DUE

DEC 19 1997		
MAR 23 1998		
APR 06 1998		
APR 27 1998		
NOV 16 1998		
APR 3 0 '09		
GAYLORD		PRINTED IN U S

THE BEGINNER'S GUIDE TO
PAPERCRAFTS

THE BEGINNER'S GUIDE TO
PAPERCRAFTS

The following paper sizes are used throughout this book:

	mm	inches
A1	841 x 594	$33\frac{1}{8}$ x $23\frac{3}{8}$
A2	594 x 420	$23\frac{3}{8}$ x $16\frac{1}{2}$
A3	420 x 297	$16\frac{1}{2}$ x $11\frac{11}{16}$
A4	297 x 210	$11\frac{11}{16}$ x $8\frac{1}{4}$
A5	210 x 148	$8\frac{1}{4}$ x $5\frac{13}{16}$

Copyright © RCS Rizzoli Libri 1995

Published by Longmeadow Press,
201 High Ridge Road, Stamford,
CT 06904, USA

Editorial and design: Brown Packaging Ltd,
255-257 Liverpool Road, London N1 1LX

ISBN: 0 681 10355 8

Material previously published in 1992 as part of the
encyclopedia set *Be Creative (*Fabbri Publishing Ltd)

Printed in The Slovak Republic

First Longmeadow Press Edition

0 9 8 7 6 5 4 3 2 1

CONTENTS

PAPERCRAFT

POP-UP CARD

MATERIALS

For the Tower Bridge pop-up card shown *below left* you will need:

Above, good quality A2 (23⅜ x 16½in) cartridge paper; rapidograph or fine black felt-tip pen; HB pencil; eraser; size 10 and size 6 brushes; tubes of cobalt blue, black and burnt umber watercolours; palette and water jar.

Creating a dramatic, three-dimensional pop-up scene out of paper might appear to be a mysterious and magical process, but after following these step-by-step instructions for London's Tower Bridge you will find that you can go on to create your own designs for personalised pop-up cards.

The traditional craft of paper folding and cutting has recently enjoyed a popular revival and is reaching highly sophisticated levels, as can be seen in the elaborate and often humorous greetings cards and books that proliferate today. This sophistication is due largely to the rapid advancement of printing technology and finishing techniques, but similar effects can be achieved at home with simple, inexpensive equipment and a knowledge of some basic techniques.

Basic construction

The Tower Bridge scene depends on a simple pop-up construction, to which is attached the cut-out forms of Tower Bridge. Strips of paper run through the centre of the bridge to represent the road.

It is important to choose a suitable weight of paper or card for this project. The weight of paper is measured in pounds per ream (lb), or in grams per square metre (gsm). An ordinary writing paper of 80gsm (40lb) would be too thin, but a 130gsm (65lb) cartridge paper, as used here, will stand up well. A slightly thicker paper or thin card could also be used. Avoid any paper with a shiny surface as this will not hold watercolour wash and pen and ink line. Use a paper and fabric adhesive such as Copydex, as this will enable you to peel pieces apart and re-position them. It will then dry quickly and evenly, with no need for weighting or clamping.

Above, cutting mat; sharp scalpel; steel ruler; paper and fabric adhesive, such as Copydex, and spreader,.

Paper sizes

25mm = 1in

Name	Dimensions
A1	841 x 594mm
A2	594 x 420mm
A3	420 x 297mm
A4	297 x 210mm
A5	210 x 148mm
A6	148 x 105mm

Machine-made paper is produced in standard sizes that are proportionally related to one another. Depending on paper type, it is available in blocks or sold in single sheets.

A1 — 841 mm
594 mm
A2
A3
A4
A5
A6

TEMPLATES

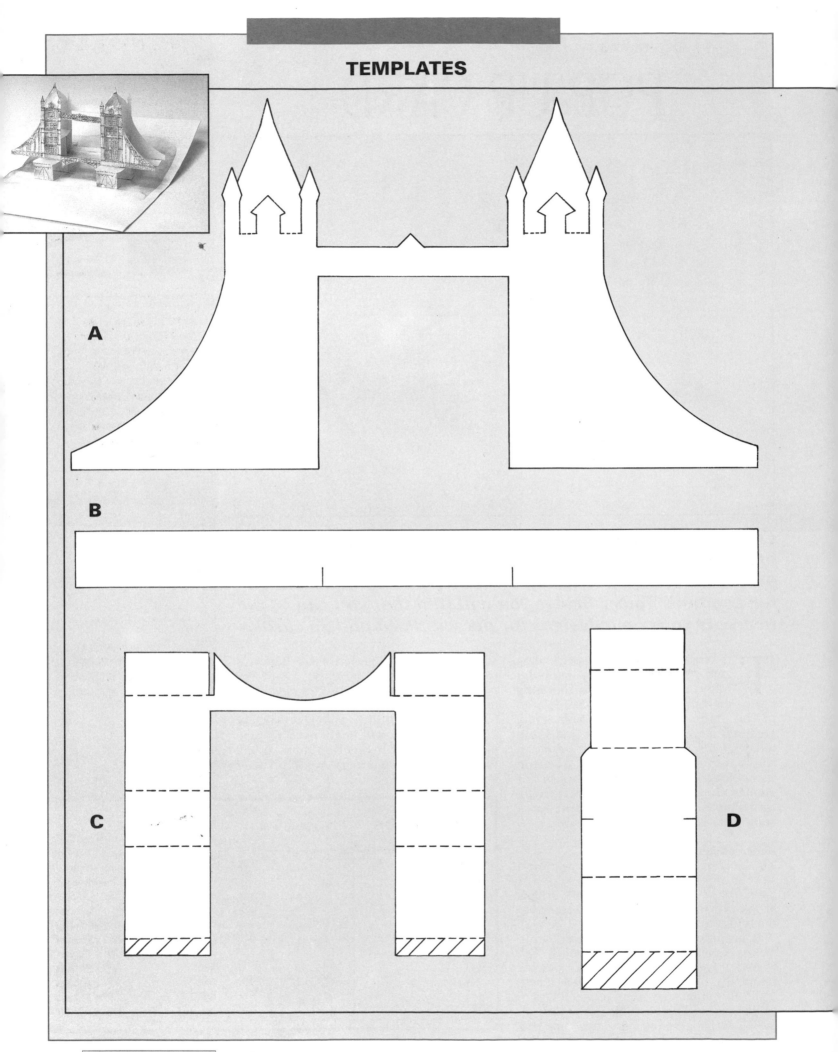

A

B

C

D

E

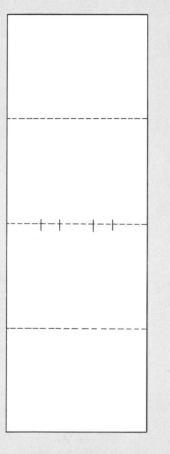

Trace off the templates shown *left* and draw the outlines in pencil on your cartridge paper. You will need two of the tower shapes (A), two roads (B), two inner supports (C) with shaded tabs and two without shaded tabs, two base supports (D) with shaded tabs and two without shaded tabs. You will also need to draw the template *above* (E) to a size of 60 x 20cm (23½ x 7⅞in), and mark the dotted fold lines at 15cm (5⅞in) intervals.

To make clean folds, score along the fold lines with the back of a scalpel blade against a metal ruler. Then turn the paper over and put the ruler behind the fold line. Fold the paper along the edge of the ruler. For the centre fold that is made inwards on the main card, score along the line on the reverse side, then fold inwards.

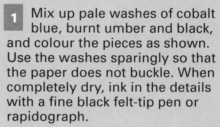

1 Mix up pale washes of cobalt blue, burnt umber and black, and colour the pieces as shown. Use the washes sparingly so that the paper does not buckle. When completely dry, ink in the details with a fine black felt-tip pen or rapidograph.

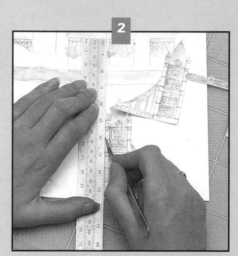

2 Put the cartridge paper on a cutting mat and cut the pieces out carefully with a sharp scalpel. Use a metal ruler as a guide for the straight edges and cut the curves freehand.

3 Carefully cut out the small turrets at the top of the main towers.

4 Using the back of the scalpel blade and the metal ruler, score along the dotted fold lines of all the cut-out pieces. It's a good idea to practise on a piece of spare paper first to make sure you don't cut right through.

5 Fold along the scored lines, as described on the previous page. To make the base supports, match up the two pairs of base pieces (one with a bottom tab is paired with one without). Spread glue on the bottom section of one of the pieces without a tab.

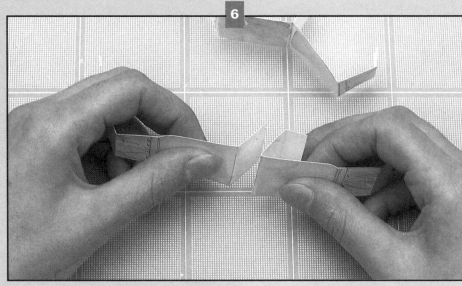

6 Glue to the corresponding section of its paired piece. Repeat with the other pair of base pieces.

7 Match up the two inner support pieces and glue them together as shown.

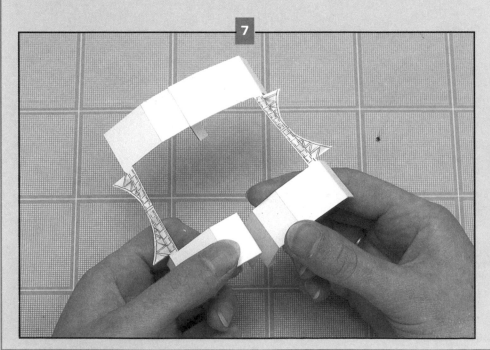

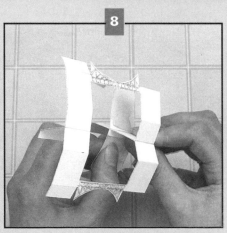

8 Apply glue to one of the bottom tabs of the inner support construction and glue to one of the base supports, matching the tab fold line to the centre join in the base support as shown. Repeat with the other tab.

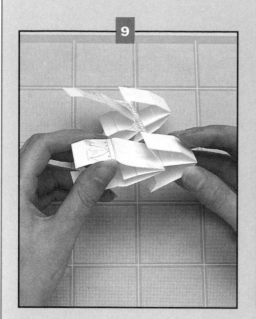

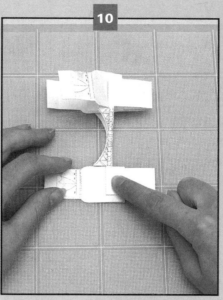

9 Fold the construction as shown.

10 Press it down so that the construction lies quite flat. This is the basic mechanism that ensures your Tower Bridge pops up when the card opens.

11 Put glue on one of the free tabs and stick down, holding the construction flat until dry. Repeat with the other three tabs. Leave to dry flat.

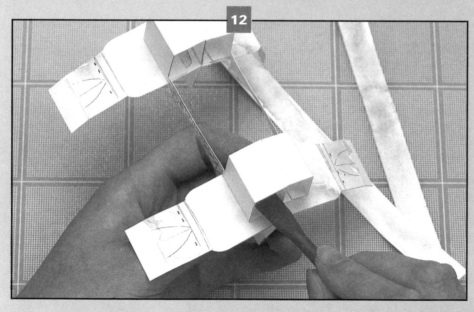

12 Open up the support construction. Apply glue to the road area under the arches.

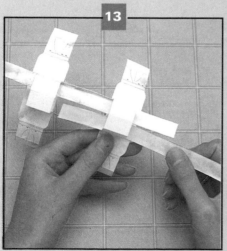

13 Carefully thread the road pieces through the arches and press down to stick.

14 Apply glue to the front of the tower supports and stick on one of the tower pieces. Turn the construction round and glue on the other tower piece.

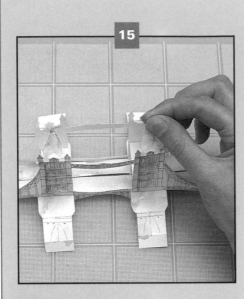

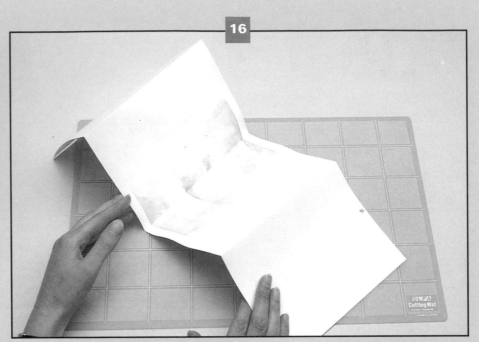

15 Carefully bend the tops of the towers back at the line shown. Apply glue to the insides of the tips of the towers and hold together until dry.

16 Paint a pale wash of cobalt blue on the large sheet of paper as shown. Leave to dry. Fold upwards at the centre fold, and downwards at the other folds.

17 Put the paper painted side down and fold down each end to the centre. Apply glue to the inner surface of the folded down pieces and press down firmly.

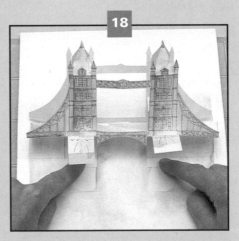

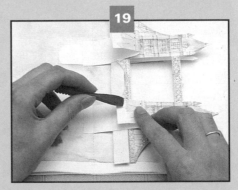

18 Turn the card over. Take the bridge construction and glue the two centre tabs to align with the centre fold of the card.

19 Fold the bridge flat and apply glue to the two front tabs. Fold the lefthand side of the card over on top of the flattened bridge construction and leave to dry. Then repeat with the rear tabs. Leave to dry folded flat under a heavy book.

Now that you have made your Tower Bridge pop-up card you can apply the basic 'pop-up' construction to make a card of any famous building, such as St Paul's Cathedral or the Eiffel Tower.

PAPERCRAFT

CAROUSEL BOX

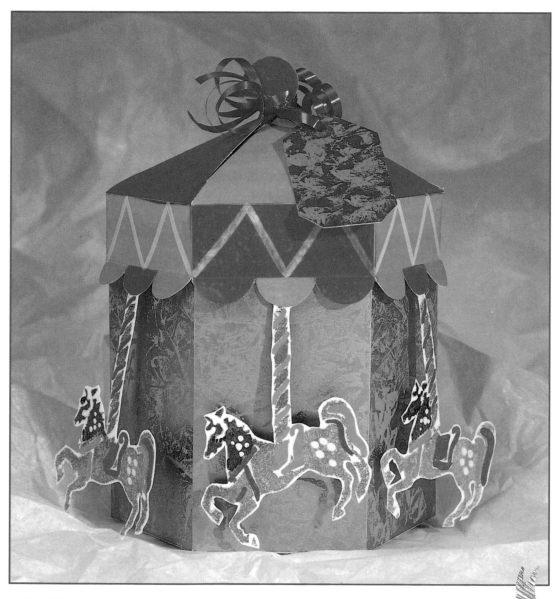

MATERIALS

To make the gift box shown *below left* you will need:

Above, sheet of tracing paper; pencil; carbon paper; metal ruler; scalpel; gold card, 510 x 340mm (20 x 13½in); white card 510 x 340mm (20 x 13½in); cutting board or piece of formica offcut; scissors.

Above, four tubes of designers gouache in Cyprus green, jet black, permanent white and rose tyrien; compass; clear adhesive book-covering film; PVA (white) glue; small rag; No 6 paint brush; white plate; A4 (11¹¹⁄₁₆ x 8¼in) sheet of stencil card or thin plain card.

The fairground was the inspiration for this charming carousel gift box. Made from only two sheets of card and some paint, it will extend your skills in the fascinating craft known as paper engineering.

Paper engineering is the technical term for making three-dimensional objects out of paper and card. We have already introduced you to the craft with the pop-up card project of London's Tower Bridge. You can see many examples of ingenious folding and cutting of paper and card in everyday life — from the simple cardboard box of the supermarket to the sleek packaging used for perfumes and toiletries. Any of these can be a source of inspiration for creating your own beautiful gift boxes and other useful containers.

In making our carousel box you will put into practice the basic scoring, folding and

tucking techniques most often used in paper engineering. Scoring is achieved by lightly running a sharp craft knife or scalpel along the edge of a steel ruler, so that the card is not cut through completely. An example of tucking can be found on any cereal packet, where the opening and closing flap at the top of the box is slotted into the ready-cut slit.

We have used rag rolling to add decoration to the gold card forming the base of the box, and stencils to create the horses and poles. Both are simple and effective techniques that you can employ to produce texture and repeat an image.

USING THE TEMPLATE

Trace the templates for the pole and horse on to a piece of tracing paper. Put a piece of carbon paper (carbon side down) between your tracing and a piece of stencil or plain card and go over the designs with a pencil.

1 Carefully cut out the stencils for the pole and horse with a scalpel.

HELPFUL HINT

When cutting the stencils, cut along the outside of the pencil lines; if you cut on the inside of the line the stencilling area will be smaller. To control the scalpel blade and prevent it from slipping, place your index finger on the side of the blade as you cut. When working on the detailed parts of the stencil, such as the horse's head and tail, turn the stencil card as you cut, instead of moving the scalpel around the curves.

2 To make the base of the gift box, draw a rectangle 215 x 450mm (8½ x 17¾in) on the gold card and divide it into the sections shown in diagram 1. (You can use a set square for this.) Draw a flap 10mm (⅜in) wide along the edge of the righthand rectangle.

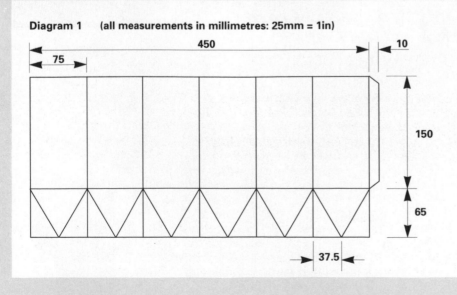

Diagram 1 (all measurements in millimetres: 25mm = 1in)

450
10
75
150
65
37.5

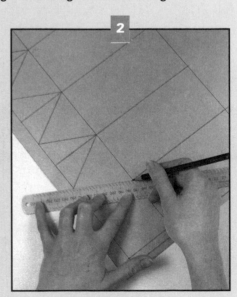

3 Mix up equal parts of green and white paint with a drop of water until the paint is the consistency of single cream. Roll up a small piece of rag approximately 200 x 500mm (8 x 20in) and scrunch it into a ball. Dip the rag into the paint. Practise making a few prints on a piece of scrap paper, until the paint disperses to give a fairly even texture. Apply the paint by dabbing the rag in a straight up-and-down movement.

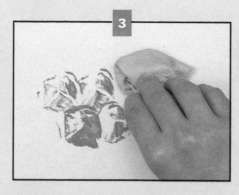

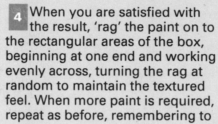

4 When you are satisfied with the result, 'rag' the paint on to the rectangular areas of the box, beginning at one end and working evenly across, turning the rag at random to maintain the textured feel. When more paint is required, repeat as before, remembering to

make a test print first. It does not matter if you get some paint on the section where you have drawn your triangles, as these will form the base of box and are not usually seen. However, for a neat result, remove any unwanted smudges with a damp cloth.

SCORING AND FOLDING

1 Scoring makes it easier to fold the card. With the scalpel, and using a steel ruler as a guide, lightly run down the line to be scored. Only the surface of the card should be cut — do not cut all the way through.

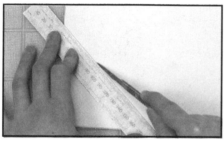

2 To fold a scored line, bend the card along the line, as if you were snapping open the scored line. You will find that the card bends and folds naturally.

Diagram 2

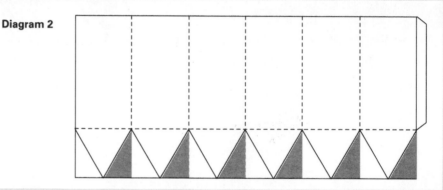

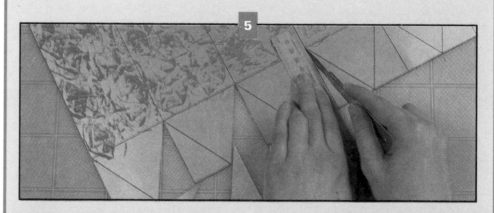

5 Using a scalpel and a steel ruler as a guide, cut out the base of the box, cutting along the outside lines of the large rectangle. Then cut out the small, righthand triangle in each of the bottom sections; these triangles are shown as the shaded portions in diagram 2. When you have cut these out you will have two triangles left below each rectangle.

6 Score along all the lines that are to be folded — the dotted lines shown in diagram 2 (see Scoring and folding *above left*).

7 Fold all the scored sections, including the line on the lefthand side of the flap, as shown.

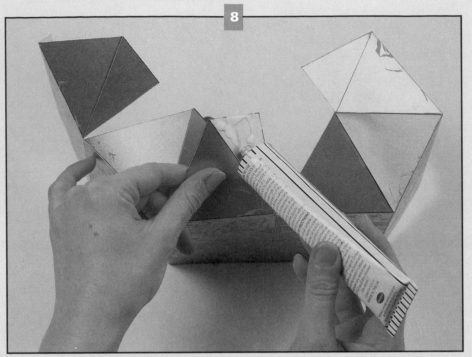

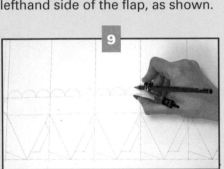

9 To make the lid, draw a rectangle 225 x 456mm (8⅞ x 18in) and divide it into the sections shown in diagram 3. Draw a flap at the lefthand end, between the two central lines. Set your compass points to a width of 12.5mm (½in) and draw three semi-circles in each of the bottom six sections, as shown. Draw two circles with a diameter of 25mm (1in) at the top.

8 To form the base of the box, apply PVA (white) glue to the righthand triangles, removing any excess glue with a cloth. Attach the glued surface to the underside of the triangle lying to its right.

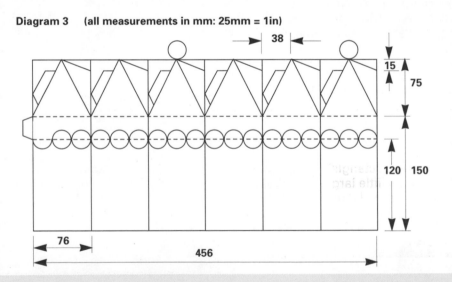

Diagram 3 (all measurements in mm: 25mm = 1in)

38
15
75
120   150
76
456

10 Mix up some white and black paint to make a grey colour. Place your horse stencil on the card in the centre of the lefthand rectangle, positioning it near the bottom line. Wrap a small piece of rag around your index finger and dip it into the paint, then rag the paint over the horse's body and tail. Put some black paint into the dish and rag the colour on to the horse's head. Carefully lift off the stencil and replace it in the adjoining rectangle, this time positioning it a little higher than in the previous rectangle. Rag on the colour as before and continue across the card, remembering to alternate the position of the stencil in each section. If you wish, you can also angle some of horses a little, as shown, but make certain that you keep them within the lines of the rectangle.

11 When you have completed the horses, position the stencil for the pole above the first horse so that it extends up to the centre of the middle semi-circle. Rag on the grey colour, as you did in Step 10, and repeat for each horse. Leave the paint to dry.

12 Squeeze some rose tyrien on to your dish and, using the No 6 brush, apply the colour to the 'roof' of the first section, as shown. In the same section, paint the centre semi-circle, the 'ribbon' on the pole, the horse's saddle and part of tail in the same colour. Mix up some green and white paint and use this to paint the remaining features in this section. Paint the rest of the lid, alternating the colours in each section. You can either paint in the white zig-zags on the border as you complete each section, or leave this until you have painted the entire lid.

13 Cut a rectangle of covering film a little larger than the size of the painted lid and apply it to the surface of the card.

14 With a pair of sharp scissors, carefully cut around the semi-circles, down the poles and around the horses. When cutting out the horses and poles, leave a thin margin of white card around them, as shown. Using diagram 4 as a guide, cut out the top section (you can use a scalpel and steel ruler for the straight lines if you wish) then score along the dotted lines in the diagram. Note that the line AB, and those above it, are scored on the right side of the card, while the line CD is scored on the reverse side. With the scalpel and ruler, cut through the lines that will take the flaps; these are shown as heavy black lines in the diagram.

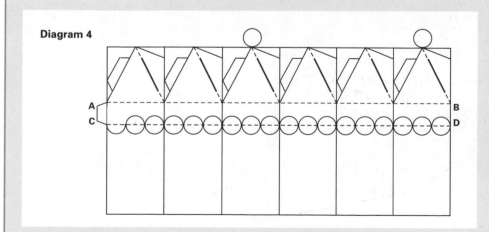

Diagram 4

HELPFUL HINT

To apply the covering film, carefully peel away the backing and lay the covering, sticky side up, on your work surface. Turn your piece of card over and lay it face down on top of the film, pressing the card gently with your fingers. Turn the card right side up and smooth out the film.

15 Fold the lid along all the scored lines and glue the side flap on the lefthand side to the back of the righthand border. To close the box, insert the flaps on the sides of the triangles through the slits.

16 Place the lid on the box, bend out the scored semi-circles and your carousel is complete.

To complete your gift box for presentation, make a matching tag out of a scrap piece of gold card and rag it to match the main part of your box. Punch a hole in one end of the tag, thread it with ribbon, and then tie the ribbon around the top of the box.

PAPERCRAFT

3-D GREETINGS CARD

MATERIALS

To make the 3-D 'get well' card shown *below* and *below left* you will need:

Above, A5 (8¼ x 5⅞in) sheet of cartridge paper, 150gsm (80lb); automatic pencil with 2B lead, size 0.5; plastic eraser; black fine-liner pen, size 0.1; felt-tipped pens, blue, green, red and yellow; scalpel and spare blade; Copydex (white) glue; sheet of blue tissue paper.

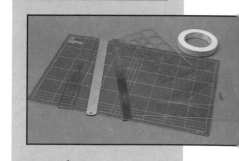

Above, cutting mat; 3 rulers (one metal); large set square; circle template; masking tape.

In the pop-up scene of Tower Bridge, you made a three-dimensional pop-up card by cutting out and gluing the pieces to a backing card. This project shows you another method of creating pop-ups, in which the design is cut from a single sheet.

Pop-ups are fascinating because they combine the disciplines of geometry and engineering with the visual magic of art and design; images can be made to appear and disappear, leap out of the page, or change into something totally different. Pop-ups have a surprisingly long history. As far back as the 15th century, illustrations of human anatomy were printed on superimposed loose leaves which could be lifted to reveal details of the muscles, skeleton and internal organs, as if the reader were observing a dissection.

A movable feast

The golden age of pop-up books and cards lasted from the 1850s until the First World War. The most inventive and humorous designs were created by the German artist Lothar Meggendorfer. His most famous books for children featured three-dimensional panoramas and amazing

movable circus and jungle scenes operated by pull-tabs, revolving discs and fold-out flaps. Pop-up production went into decline in the 1930s and was not revived until the 1960s, since when pop-up books and greetings cards have once again enjoyed enormous popularity.

Incised pop-ups

Our greetings card uses one of the simplest pop-up methods, in which a sheet of paper or card is folded and then slit and creased across the fold. When the card is opened out to 90º, giving a horizontal and vertical plane, the overlapping layers inside are revealed. The beauty of this method is that multi-layered designs can be created from a single sheet, and no gluing is required. The imaginative possibilities are endless and you will have great fun designing cards for all occasions.

HOW THE CARD WORKS

Before starting on the project it is a good idea to practise making simple constructions like the 'box' shown *below*, following the diagram *right*.

x = depth of box   y = height of box

— · — · —	= score on the front
- - - - - - -	= score on reverse
————	= cut

Mark the centre fold line and the required width of the box. On the left, mark the required height of the box **y** above the centre line as shown. On the right mark the required depth of the box **x** below the centre line as shown. Now mark off **y** and **x** from the bottom and top lines as shown. Cut and score as indicated, and fold along the centre line to form the box.

MULTI-LAYERED DESIGNS

These examples show how complex, multi-layered designs can be developed from the basic idea of the incised 'box' *left*, on which our project card is based.

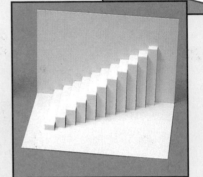

THE TEMPLATE

black — cut lines
pink — score on the back
blue — score on the front

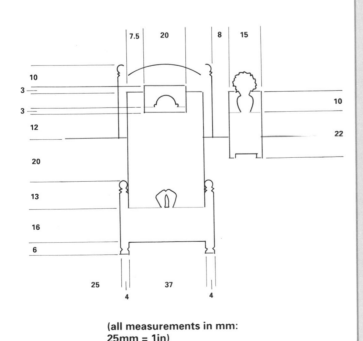

(all measurements in mm:
25mm = 1in)

DRAWING PARALLEL LINES

To help you draw the parallel lines of the diagram accurately, we show you *below* how to set up a simple version of the parallel motion board used by designers and draftsmen. Take two rulers and lay them on the cutting mat as shown, one aligned horizontally and one vertically to form a right-angled corner (make sure the rulers align perfectly with the horizontal and vertical lines marked on the cutting mat). Secure the rulers to the mat with masking tape so they stay firmly in place. Lay the set square in place with the two straight edges butting up against the rulers. When you draw up the diagram (see step 2), slide the set square along the two rulers to position the lines.

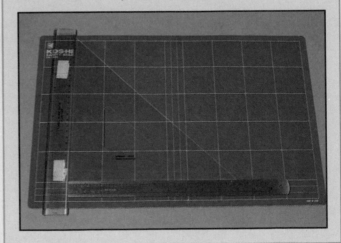

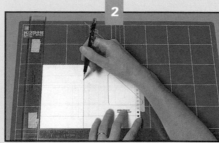

1 On the sheet of A5 (8¼ x 5⅞in) paper draw a rectangle 200 x 120mm (7⅞ x 4¾in), making sure the corners are perfect right angles. Mark the centre fold of the card with a dashed line (to avoid confusion when you draw the lines of the design later).

2 Position the paper between the two rulers on your 'parallel motion board' (see Drawing parallel lines box, *opposite*). Secure with masking tape. Copy the template, following the measurements given. Draw the lines lightly so that you can erase them later.

3 When the initial diagram is complete, remove the paper from the board. Using the 4mm (⁵⁄₃₂in) circle on the circle template, draw the four knobs on top of the bed posts. Draw the top three-quarters of the circle only — not the complete circle.

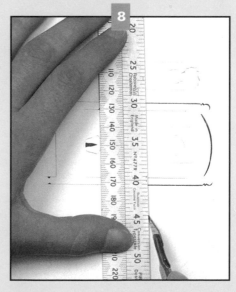

5 Now draw the boy's head and feet, and the bedside cabinet. For the head, use the 10mm (⅜in) circle on the circle template to draw a semi-circle centred on the line indicated. Draw the feet (about 8mm (¼in) high), also centred on the line indicated. Draw the bedside cabinet and the vase of flowers. With the fine-liner pen draw the boy's features, indicate the toes, and draw the flower stalks and the cabinet door and drawer.

4 Draw tiny V-shapes to form the 'notches' below the bedknobs (for the knobs on the bedhead, draw these V-shapes on the outer edges only). Make tiny V-shaped cuts to form the shapes of the feet of the bed.

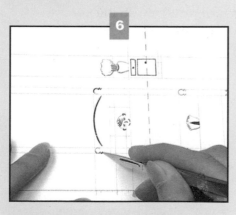

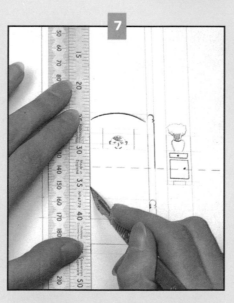

6 Find the centre of the line of the top of the bedhead and draw a crescent shape as shown. With the scalpel, start cutting out the design (see template for which lines to cut). Start by cutting the intricate shapes (the bed posts, the outlines of the head and feet and the vase of flowers). When cutting the shape of the bedhead cut two lines very

close together and remove a slither of paper; when the card is opened up the light will shine through these lines from the back.

7 Now cut along all the straight lines using the scalpel held against a metal ruler. Again follow the diagram carefully so that you don't cut any lines by mistake.

8 Score along all the front score lines shown on the diagram; do this by running the 'blunt' edge of the scalpel blade along the edge of a steel ruler to make a slight indent in the paper. With the point of the scalpel, pierce the ends of the back score lines, then turn the card over and score the lines, using the marks as guidelines.

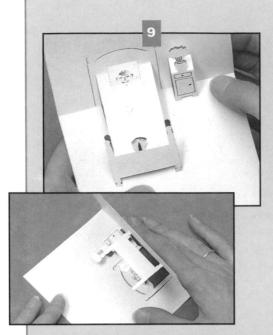

9 Cut away the excess from around the card and erase the pencil guidelines. Start to gently ease out the shapes of the bed and the cupboard by running your fingernail along each of the score lines and then gently bending them in the direction in which they were scored. Score and bend the centre fold line of the card. Fold up the card and press flat to reinforce the creases (see inset).

WEDDING AND BABY CARDS

Below we give templates for the 'wedding' and 'baby' congratulations cards shown together with the 'get well' card in the main picture . Photocopy them to the required size, transfer on to card and construct in the same way as the project card. Decorate them as you wish.

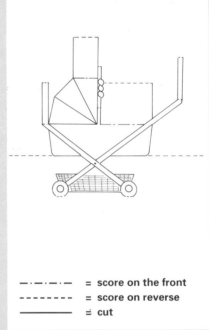

—·—·—·— = score on the front

– – – – – – = score on reverse

——————— = cut

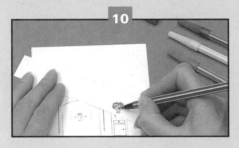

10 Open the card and lay it flat. Slip a scrap of paper under the flowers on the cut-out shape of the flowers and colour them with red, yellow and blue felt-tipped pens.

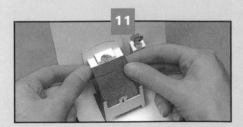

11 To make the bed cover, cut out a piece of tissue paper 55mm (2⅛in) square and crumple slightly. Fold over 10mm (⅜in) at one end. Smear glue over the top of the bed, then lay the tissue paper over it and tuck the edges under.

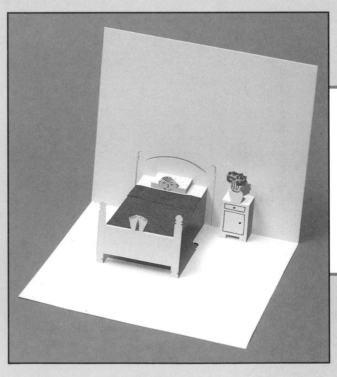

If you place your pop-up card on a windowsill or in front of a table lamp, the light will shine through the incised lines, adding even more to the magical effect.

PAPER LAMPSHADE

Further your skills in paper engineering with this lampshade for a child's bedroom. Inspired by the nursery rhyme 'There was an old woman who lived in a shoe', it is designed to be used with a papier mâché lamp base that is the subject of a later project.

O ur paper lampshade is constructed from thin card and is supported by a wire frame. The pyramid shape forms the 'roof' of the boot, in which the Old Woman kept so many children — step-by-step instructions for the boot lamp base are featured in a later project. However, the lampshade could also be used with a simple ceramic base, if you wish.

We begin the lesson by showing you how to construct the three-dimensional shape from a single piece of card with very basic equipment — a pair of compasses, a ruler and a pencil. The materials you will need to make the wire frame include solder, a soldering iron and a pair of pliers. The lampshade will be perfectly safe to use as long as you follow the instructions given in the lesson and take the normal sensible precautions that you would with any item

that is used in a child's room. For the light bulb, use either an 8-watt night light or a mini fluorescent bulb, both of which will fit a standard bayonet lamp fitting. We also recommend that you spray the lampshade with a flame retardant spray such as Flambar 53, following the manufacturer's instructions carefully. This can be purchased from specialist hardware stores.

HELPFUL HINT

Before you begin the soldering, carefully wipe the surfaces of the wire with a soft, clean cloth to remove any dirt and dust, as this will prevent the solder from adhering properly to the wire and the join will not be sufficiently strong.

MATERIALS

To make the paper lampshade shown *below left* you will need:

Above, one sheet of thin card in a light colour such as champagne, 500 x 500mm (20 x 20in); pair of compasses; scalpel; fibre-tip pen; strong, quick-drying adhesive, such as Impact; steel ruler; long plastic ruler; eraser; cutting board.

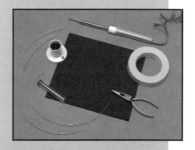

Above, fine emery paper; masking tape; soldering iron; solder; lamp holder; two 500mm (20in) lengths of galvanised wire, 1.6mm (¹/₁₆ in) thick; pliers.

Above, dish, or palette; tracing paper; jam jar; fine-tip pen; artist's watercolour paints in cobalt blue, vermilion, hooker's green dark, scarlet red and cadmium yellow pale; size 1 artist's brush.

TEMPLATE

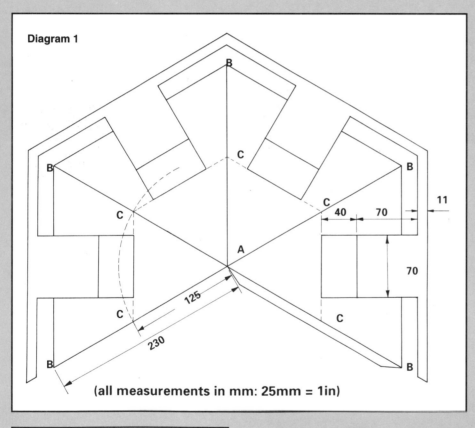

Diagram 1

11

40 70

70

125

230

(all measurements in mm: 25mm = 1in)

Diagram 2

60°

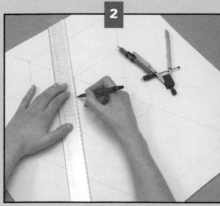

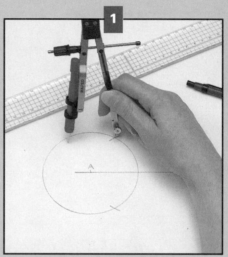

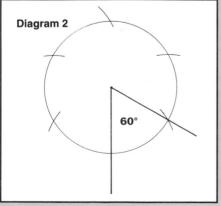

1 Using diagram **1** as a guide, construct the shape of the lampshade, drawing all the lines lightly with a pencil as they will be erased later. First mark the centre point A, which is at least 250mm (10in) from each edge of the card. Draw the vertical AB and then construct four 60° angles at point A as shown (see diagram **2** for constructing a 60° angle with a pair of compasses).

2 The lines AB are the lines of these angles, and are each 230mm (9in) long. Join points B to form the base line of the lampshade. Draw an arc from point A with the compasses set at 125mm (5in). The arc cuts through the lines AB at points C. Join points C together, as shown. This line will be the top of the window sections.

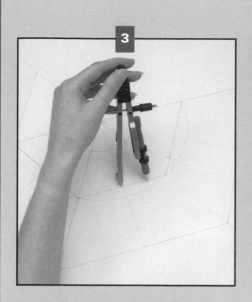

3 Divide each of the base lines (BB) in half and draw a line from each centre point to point A, making sure that your lines go below the base line. Set your compasses to 35mm (1⅜in) and mark points either side of the centre point of the base lines and of the top window lines, as shown. Join the points you have marked to form the sides of the window sections.

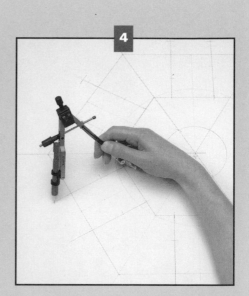

4 From the top of the window, make marks down each side line at 40mm (1⅝in), 110mm (4⁵⁄₁₆in) and 121mm (4¾in).

5 Using the points you have just marked, complete the drawing of each section (see diagram **3**).

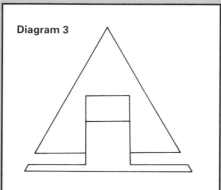

Diagram 3

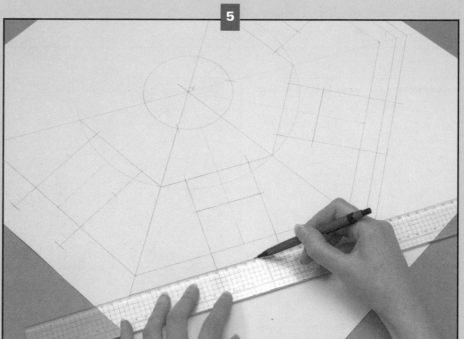

6 Draw a 10 mm (⅜in) wide tab on one of the end sections (see diagram **1**).

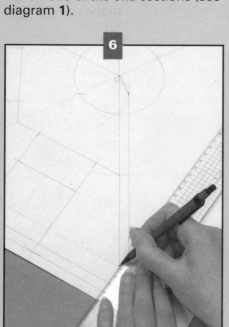

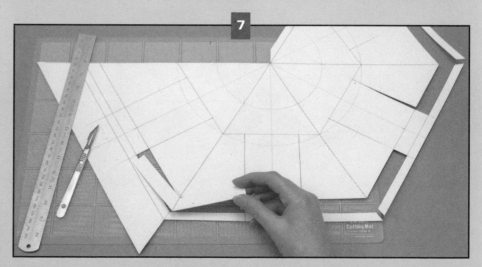

7 Cut out the complete shape of the lampshade (see diagram **4**). The long pieces at the bottom will form tabs when the shape is assembled. Cut 5mm (³⁄₁₆in) off each end of these tabs, making the cut parallel to the original line.

Diagram 4

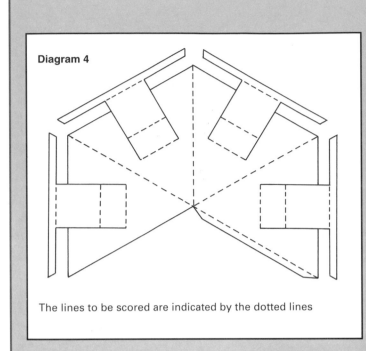

The lines to be scored are indicated by the dotted lines

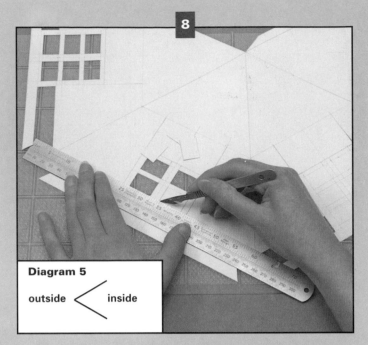

Diagram 5

outside < inside

Diagram 6 (all measurements in mm: 25mm = 1in)

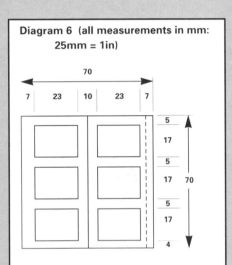

8 Score all the lines shown as dotted lines in diagram **4**. Score lines should always be made on the outside of a fold. This means that some lines should be scored on the reverse of the card. Look at the picture of the final object to see which way the sections should fold, and also diagram **5**. Draw on the window panes using the measurements in diagram **6** and cut out each pane. One window should be opened; the dotted lines in diagram **6** indicate where it should be scored.

9 Rub out all the pencil lines and fold the lampshade along the scored lines.

10 Glue the base tabs and stick them to the underside of the shade, as shown, aligning them with the base of the shade.

11 Glue the main tab to form the pyramid shape.

Diagram 7

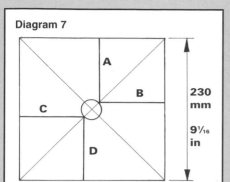

The diameter of the circle is 28mm (1⅛in). **Draw the lines A, B, C and D from the circle parallel to the sides of the large square.**

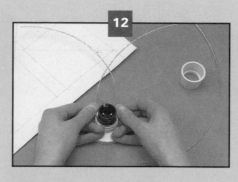

12 Cut two pieces of galvanised wire 500mm (19¾in) in length. Draw the frame plan (see diagram 7). Bend each piece of wire from the centre, halfway around the lamp holder, as shown.

13 Place one piece of wire on the frame plan so that the top of the loop sits on the centre circle of the plan. With a pencil, mark the wire at the two points where it meets the intersection of lines A and B, and C and D, as shown.

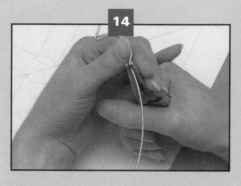

14 Using a pair of pliers, bend the wire outwards at the marked points. Repeat Step 13 with the other piece of wire, then place both pieces on the frame plan.

15 Straighten the wires so that they lie along lines A, B, C and D. Mark the points at which the wires cross the outside lines of the frame plan and bend at these points so that the wires form two squares.

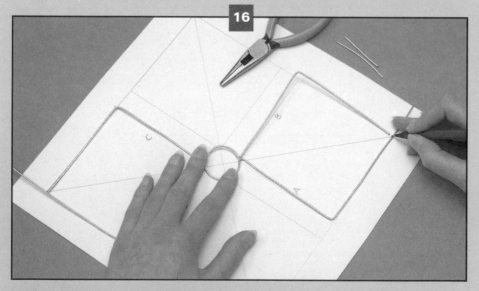

16 Mark the points at which the ends of the two sections meet and cut off the excess with the 'snipping' part of the pliers.

17 Draw a right angle on a piece of spare card and cut the corner off, as shown in diagram 8.

Tape the card to your work surface so that the cut corner hangs over the edge. Tape the two wires to the card so that the ends meet. Heat the soldering iron for a few minutes. When it is hot, apply the solder to the ends of wire and solder the ends together, as shown.

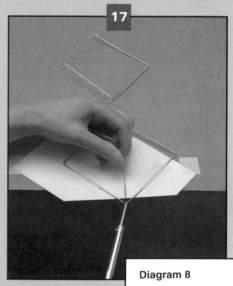

Repeat with the other end of the wire frame. File the soldering with fine emery paper.

Diagram 8

a piece of scrap card

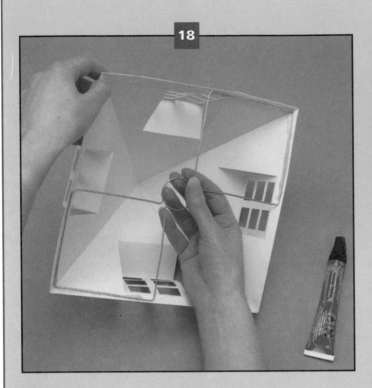

18 Turn the lampshade upside-down and glue along the edges of the two corners with a strong adhesive. Place the frame in position and hold it between your fingers until dry. Put masking tape over the wire to give a neat finish.

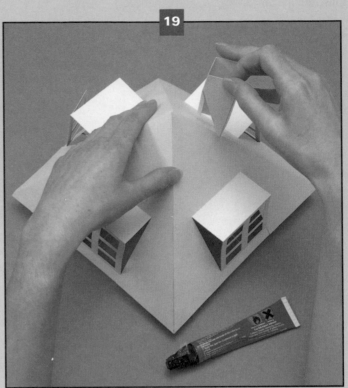

19 Construct the chimney, referring to diagram **9**. Cut away the shaded area and score along the dotted lines. Glue the tab and then glue to the lampshade.

Diagram 9   (all measurements in mm: 25mm = 1in)

70

19

30

120

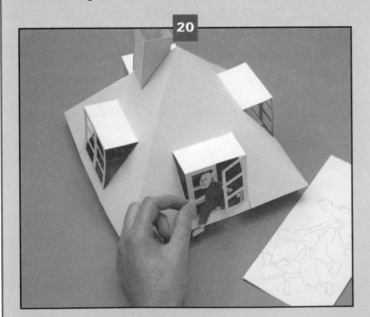

20 Photocopy the template of the four children at 140% and trace it on a piece of scrap card. Paint in the children's clothes with a size 1 paint brush and watercolour paints. Leave to dry. Using a fine tipped black pen define the face and other details. Cut the characters out and glue the single character in place, half way through the open window. Glue the other children to the side of the chimney and window section.

Our next paper project will show you how to make the Old Woman's shoe that housed so many children she didn't know what to do!
  Put together, the two make an amusing nursery rhyme lamp for a child's bedroom.

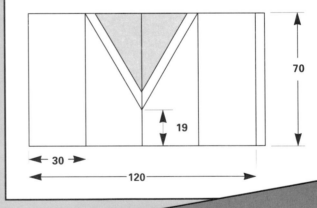

PAPERCRAFT

STATIONERY BOX

Above, book cloth, 500 x 600mm (20 x 24in); 1.5mm (¹⁄₁₆in)-thick millboard, 500 x 500mm (20 x 20in); marbled paper, 297 x 420mm (12 x 20in) 13mm (½in) split pin.

Above, cutting board; set square; steel ruler; pencil; PVA (white) glue; clear adhesive glue, such as Bostik; scissors; craft knife; scalpel; bone folder; jam jar; scrap paper; 25mm (1in) decorator's brush; single hole punch, or bradawl and hammer.

This elegant stationery box would make a delightful gift, particularly if you filled it with your own handmade paper. We show you how to make it from simple materials, using sophisticated cutting, folding and gluing techniques that will ensure a highly professional finish.

Some of the techniques used for this project are similar to those used in making the carousel box, and we shall also be introducing you to some more advanced techniques.

The main materials you will need for the stationery box are book cloth and millboard. Millboard comes in different weights and is sold by its thickness in millimeters or inches. We have used 1.5mm (¹⁄₁₆in) board for this project.

Finding the grain
All paper and card is made up of fibres that become aligned in the same direction during the manufacturing process. This alignment is known as the direction of the grain. To determine the grain of your millboard, hold two of the opposite edges in either hand and bend the board slightly; if it is resistant to bending, you are bending against the grain. If you bend it by holding the other two edges it should 'give' more easily because you are bending with the grain. Mark the direction of the grain on your piece of board with an arrow.

Having determined the direction of the grain, you should take it into consideration when drawing your shapes for the box. The long thin pieces (A, B and C) should be drawn and cut with the grain running along them; this will prevent the board from warping unnecessarily when you have completed your box.

THE DIAGRAM

This diagram shows all the shapes you need to draw and cut out in step 1. Shapes A to G are used for the box itself; shapes H and I are used to make the fastener. When drawing the shapes on your piece of millboard, make certain your measurements are accurate and that pieces A, B, C, F and G lie along the grain of the board (see previous page).

(all measurements in millimetres: 25mm = 1in)

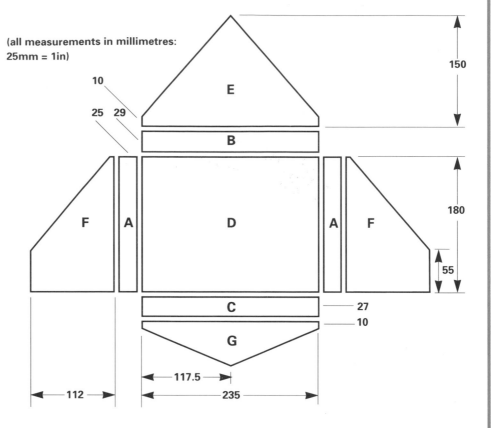

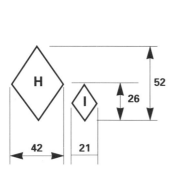

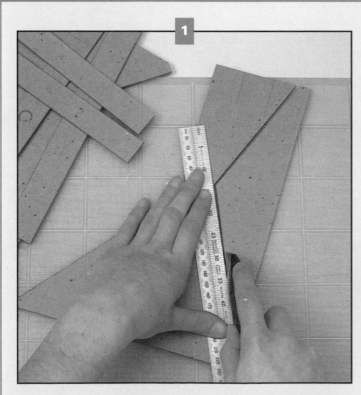

1 Using a set square, steel ruler and pencil, draw each of the shapes shown in the diagram *above* on a piece of millboard. Mark each shape with the letter corresponding to its letter in the diagram. Cut out the shapes with a craft knife, using a steel rule as a guide. You will have to cut over the lines several times in order to cut completely through the millboard.

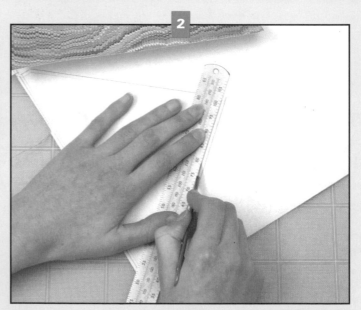

2 For the lining, place a piece of marbled paper on the cutting board, wrong side facing you, and position pieces E, G, D and F on the paper, making sure that one edge of each shape is parallel with the edge of the paper (and so parallel with the grain). Draw around each shape with a pencil. Remove the shapes and draw another set of lines 3mm (⅛in) inside the first, as shown. Cut out the shapes with a scalpel, cutting along the inside lines. Using piece E, cut the piece of paper to decorate the front flap, following the instructions in the box *right*. Set the cut-out shapes of marbled paper to one side.

DECORATIVE FRONT FLAP

1 Draw around piece E and mark the centre of the longest edge on your paper. Draw a line from this point to the top of the shape. Mark another point 140mm (5½in) along the line as shown.

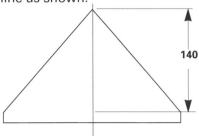

2 Turn piece E (the shaded piece) upside down and align with the line drawn on the paper. Draw around E again.

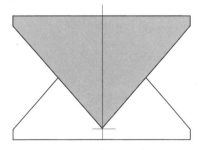

3 Draw a line 20mm(¾in) from both of the diagonal lines you have just drawn, as shown.

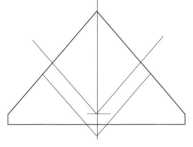

4 Cut out the front flap to give you a piece of paper shaped as below.

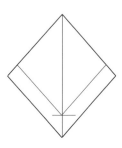

3 Place the book cloth face down on your work surface and position your millboard shapes on the cloth in the order they appear in the diagram opposite. Leave a margin of 3mm (⅛in) between the pieces, as shown. Draw around each shape with a pencil. Remove the pieces of millboard.

5 Use PVA (white) glue to glue the millboard shapes to the book cloth. Glue one shape at a time, starting with the centre rectangle. Apply the glue to the cloth, keeping the glue inside the pencil lines. Hold the brush vertically and dab the brush on to the cloth in a straight up-and-down movement. Place the millboard on top of the glued area, making certain it lies within the pencil lines before pressing it on to the cloth. Glue the small strip to the left of the rectangle next, then the strip to the right. Complete the gluing, moving outwards as you work.

HELPFUL HINT

As you glue each shape to the cloth, measure the space between it and the adjoining shape to make sure it is still 3mm (⅛in). If your cloth stretches your guide lines will not be accurate. If the space is less than 3mm (⅛in) the box will not fold properly.

4 Draw another line around the outside of the whole shape, 20mm (¾in) from the edge, as shown. (This forms the 'tabs' on the outside of each section.) Place the cloth on a cutting board and cut around the perimeter with a scalpel. Put all the scrap pieces to one side for use later.

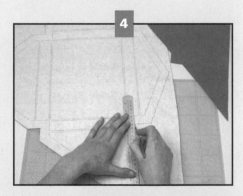

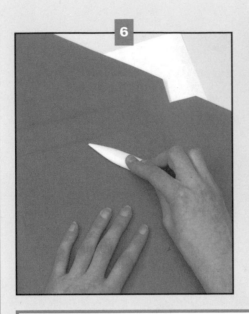

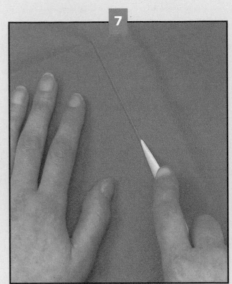

6 When you have glued down all the pieces turn the cloth over. Hold the bone folder flat against the cloth and push it over the surface — working outwards from the centre of each shape — to remove any air bubbles.

7 Using the edge of the bone folder, define the grooves between the millboard shapes by drawing the folder along the grooves, as shown.

8 Turn the cloth over and cut away the ends of the tabs with scissors, using the diagram *below* as a guide.

CUTTING THE CORNERS

When cutting away the corners of the cloth take the thickness of the board into account. The board used in this exercise is 1.5mm ($\frac{1}{16}$in) thick, so you should stop the cut 1.5mm ($\frac{1}{16}$in) away from the board. Draw a line from the corner of the cloth through the corner point of the board and mark equal angles as shown (that is, ensure that the angles marked **x** are the same, and the angles marked **y** are also equal). Cut away the lightly shaded area.

cloth

y

y   x

board   x

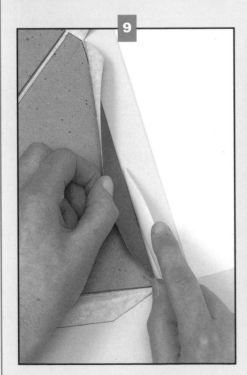

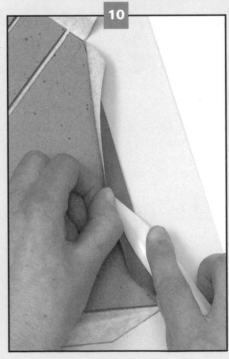

9 Place a piece of scrap paper under one of the tabs and apply PVA (white) glue to the tab, following the gluing procedure in step 5. Begin to fold the tab on to the millboard, pulling it taut with your left hand and running the bone folder along the outside edge with your right hand. Remember to use the edge of the bone folder when you are defining the edges of your work.

10 To complete the folding, hold the bone folder flat and push it over the book cloth, pushing it from the edge inwards, as shown, so that the tab adheres to the board.

11 Cut four pieces of book cloth from the scrap pieces, two measuring 232 x 60mm (9⅛ x 2⅜ in) and two 177 x 60mm (7 x 2⅜ in). Glue the back of each piece and stick centrally over each of the strips surrounding the rectangle. Define the grooves between the strips with the bone folder.

12 Glue the back of the marbled paper that will decorate the front flap, using PVA (white) glue. With the inside of the box facing you, place the paper under the flap, aligning the inside pencil lines with the edge of the flap, as shown. Turn the box over and rub the paper down with the bone folder.

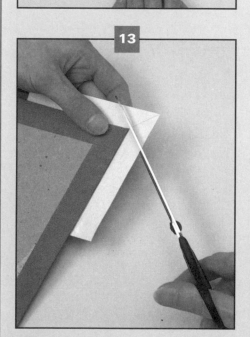

13 Cut off the tip of the marbled paper, as shown. Apply glue to the remaining tabs and fold over on to the box. Use the bone folder to smooth the surface and crease the edges.

14 Glue the lining to the inside of the box. When gluing the paper make certain it does not move, otherwise you will get glue on the front of the paper. Smooth out the lining with the bone folder.

15 Fold up the box. With a pencil, mark the shape of the bottom flap on the side flaps, and apply a clear adhesive glue to this area, as shown. Hold the flaps in place for a few minutes until the glue dries.

16 To make the fastener, place shapes H and I on a scrap of book cloth and draw round them. Then draw a line 15mm (⅝in) from each edge. Cut out the pieces of cloth, glue the millboard in the centre and smooth out the surface with the bone folder. Cut off the four corners of each shape, apply PVA (white) glue to the tabs and fold them over. Define the edges with the bone folder.

17 With the wrong sides facing you, place the smaller piece on top of the larger one, as shown. Place the hole punch in the centre of the smaller piece and punch a hole through both pieces. Turn over and put a split pin through the hole.

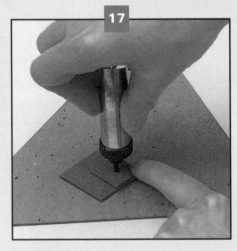

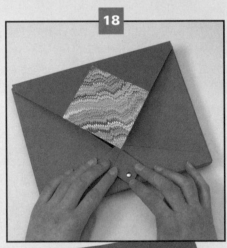

18 Using the clear adhesive, glue the fastener to the bottom flap of the box, centring it in the middle and aligning one of the corners with the edge of the box. Hold firmly in place until the glue has dried.

Book cloth is available in a number of different colours, and there is a wide range of marbled paper available. However, as marbled paper is expensive you could cut costs by using a piece of gift wrap to line your box and to decorate the front flap.

PAPERCRAFT

WINDOW BLIND

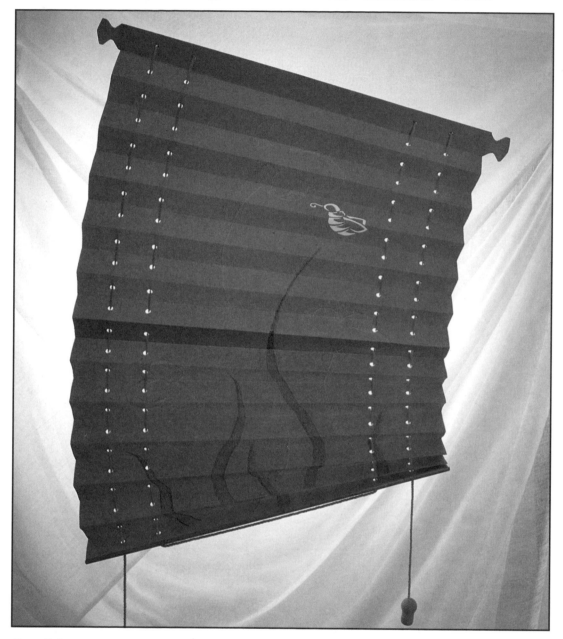

In this project we use a simple paper-folding technique to make a decorative concertina window blind that will let daylight diffuse gently into your room.

The concertina window blind that we have made is operated by a cord action and will fit a small narrow window. You can change the dimensions of the blind, but don't attempt anything much larger to begin with, and make sure that the sheets of paper are neatly joined along the fold. You could also vary the interval of the folds, or treat the decoration differently.

It is important to use strong paper that will stand up to use and withstand being immersed in dye. We have used a machine-made paper that is available in most art shops, but if you prefer a different paper, check whether it will be strong enough.

HELPFUL HINT

Choose a soft-textured cotton piping cord or a cord with a silky finish, as this will minimise the possibility of any wear and tear on the holes at the edge of the blind. Piping cord can be purchased from haberdashery shops and department stores.

MATERIALS

To make a blind to fit a window 500 x 680mm (20 x 27in) you will need:

Above, two sheets of Fabriano 5 paper, 500 x 640mm (20 x 25in); two pieces of ramin half-round wood, one 35 x 500mm (1³⁄₈ x 20in) and one 35 x 570mm (1³⁄₈ x 22½in); 6m (6½yds) of cotton piping cord, size 01; two light pulls; hole reinforcements.

Above, three tins of Dylon cold water fabric dye in moon blue; Caran d'Ache oil crayons in yellow (10) and green (229); masking fluid; size 1 paint brush; decorator's brush; thick blue pantone marker, no 229; matt varnish.

Above, pencil; thick black marker pen; long ruler; steel ruler; bone folder; PVA (white) glue; strong impact glue; coping saw; sand paper, medium grade; hand drill and 5mm (³⁄₁₆in) bit; scissors; single hole punch; masking tape; light box (see overleaf); eraser; G-clamp; scalpel; piece of thick scrap cardboard.

TEMPLATES

1

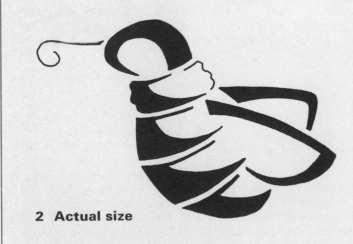

2 Actual size

Cut two sheets of paper 500 x 455mm (19¾ x 18in)
each, trimming off any watermarks. On both
sheets, mark off every 35mm (1⅜in) along the shortest
edge. On your first sheet, use a ruler and pencil to join
the first two points; on your second sheet, join the first
two and last two points (see diagram **1** *below*).

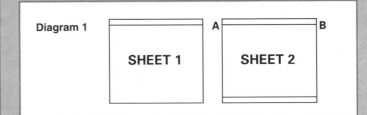

Diagram 1

SHEET 1   SHEET 2

A   B

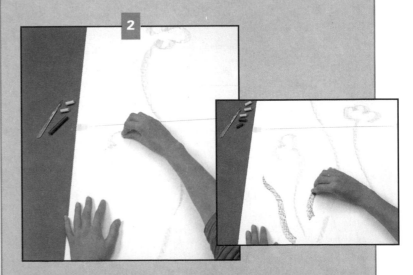

Photocopy template **1** at 200%, enlarge again to
200%, and then again to 140%. Photocopy template
2. Go over the lines with a thick black marker pen. Join
the two sheets for the blind together with masking tape
so that the bottom of sheet 1 aligns with line AB of
sheet 2. Position over template **1**. Cut the crayons into
thirds. Using the edge of the crayons, draw over the
guide lines with continuous strokes.

3 Place the template of the bee on a light box and secure it with masking tape. Position sheet 1 on top so that the bee is hovering around the flower. With a pencil, lightly draw the shape on to the sheet.

HELPFUL HINT

A light box can be improvised from a sheet of glass, two piles of books and an angle-poise lamp (see *below*).

4 Paint in the bee using masking fluid, painting slightly over the lines so that they can be rubbed out later. When the masking fluid has dried, turn the sheet over (still on the light box) and paint the bee with masking fluid on the other side.

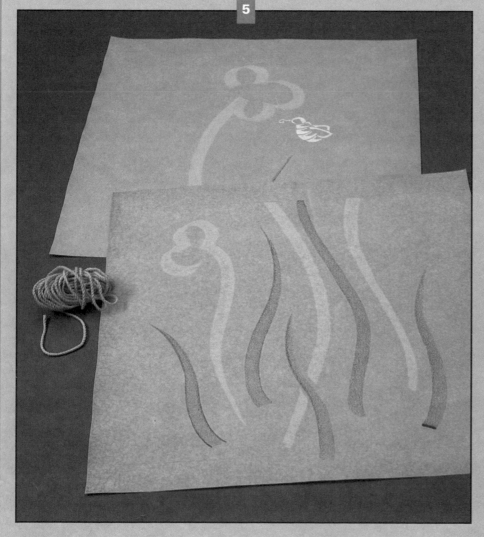

5 Separate the two sheets. Prepare the dye following the manufacturer's instructions. Put water in a bath to a depth of about 12cm (5in) – enough to cover the sheets – and add the dye. Put in the sheets of paper and leave until they reach the required colour (this may take up to 8 hours). Turn the sheets often to prevent white patches occurring. When the dye has taken, rinse the sheets with a shower attachment (they will be very delicate, so handle them carefully). To dry them, put a pad of newspaper down on a flat surface, cover with a plastic sheet and lay the paper sheets on top. Put the cord in the same dye bath and leave for 1 hour.

6 Rub out the masking fluid on the bee with your finger and erase the pencil lines.

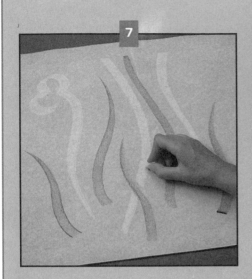

7 With the tip of the yellow crayon, put the highlights on the flowers.

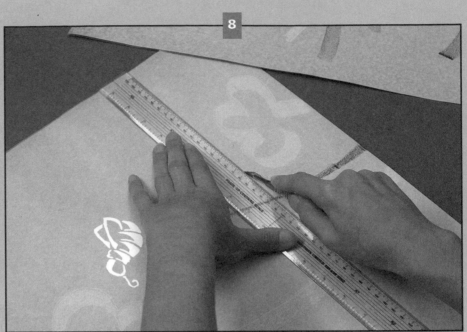

Diagram 2

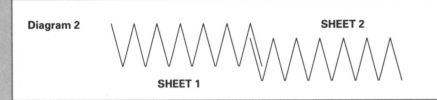

SHEET 2

SHEET 1

8 Use the 35mm (1⅜in)-interval marks you made in step 1 as guides for scoring horizontal lines. With a long ruler and the back of a scalpel blade, gently score alternate lines on one side of the paper. Turn the paper over and score the remaining lines.

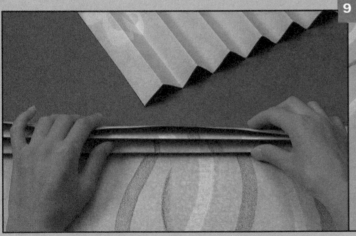

9 Fold along the lines with the scoring on the outside of the fold (see diagram **2**). Define the folds with the bone folder. Brush PVA (white) glue on to one end fold and glue the two sections together.

Diagram 3 (all measurements in mm: 25mm = 1in)

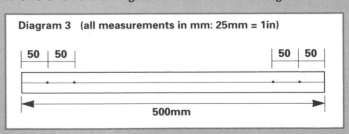

50 | 50   50 | 50

500mm

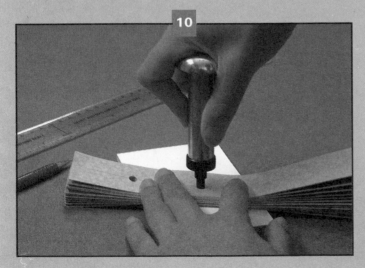

10 With the blind folded, measure 50mm (2in) and 100mm (4in) in from each end (see diagram **3**, *above*). Make four holes using the hole punch.

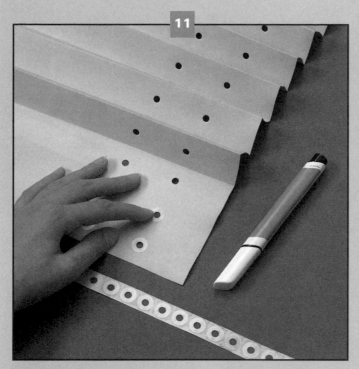

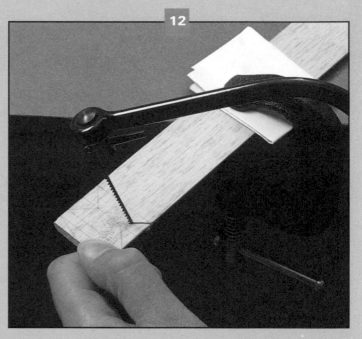

11 Using the thick blue marker, colour the hole reinforcements and leave them to dry. Put hole reinforcements on the back of each hole.

12 Clamp the 570 x 35mm (22½ x 1⅜in) piece of wood to the table with a G-clamp (put a folded piece of paper between the wood and the clamp to prevent any damage to the wood). Mark each end of the wood using diagram **4** as a guide, and then cut away the shaded areas with the coping saw.

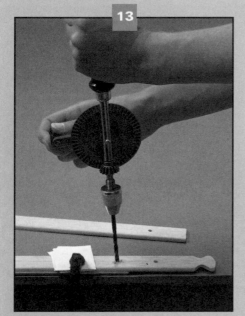

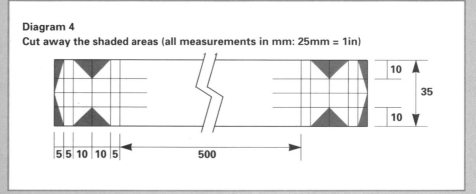

Diagram 4
Cut away the shaded areas (all measurements in mm: 25mm = 1in)

10
35
10
5 5 10 10 5
500

13 Take the 35 x 500mm (1⅜ x 20in) piece of wood and drill four holes as shown in diagram **3**. Drill the holes from the top of the wood (this will give a smooth hole on the side that will be visible). Drill corresponding holes in the other piece of wood, taking the extra length into account. Sandpaper the wood, then varnish.

14 With the strong impact glue, glue the two pieces of wood to the top and bottom of the blind.

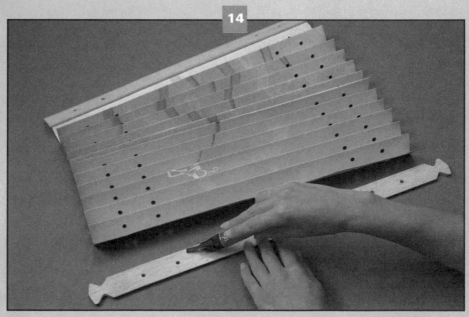

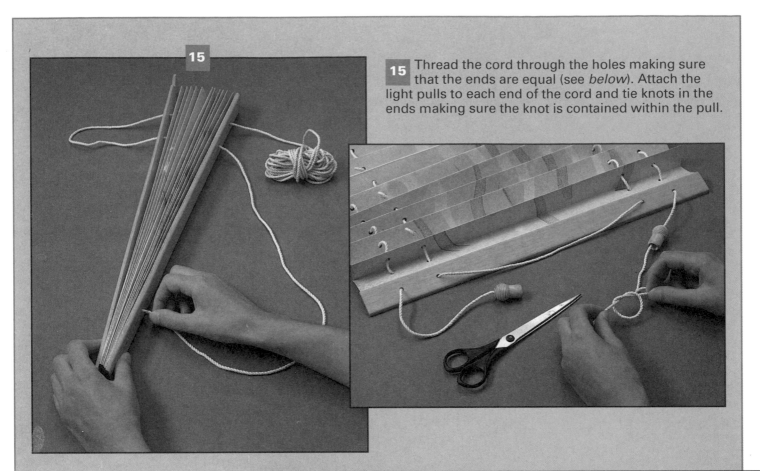

15 Thread the cord through the holes making sure that the ends are equal (see *below*). Attach the light pulls to each end of the cord and tie knots in the ends making sure the knot is contained within the pull.

Diagram 5

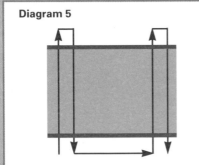

To make a blind to fit another sized window, measure your window and deduct about 80mm (3in) from the width to allow for the hanging device. The length of the blind should be about 1¹/₅ times the length of the window, as the blind always retains some of its pleating when fully extended.

To fix the blind in position, screw two cuphooks at the top of a window frame and rest the carved ends of the wood on the hooks.

To lower the blind, pull the centre loop down, and to raise the blind pull the light pulls gently outwards in a downward direction.

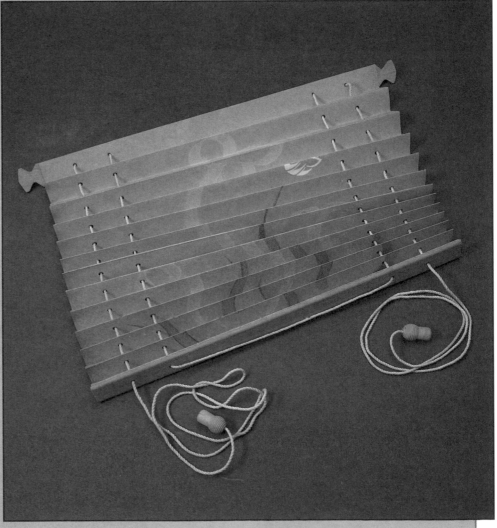

PAPERCRAFT

GIFT BAG

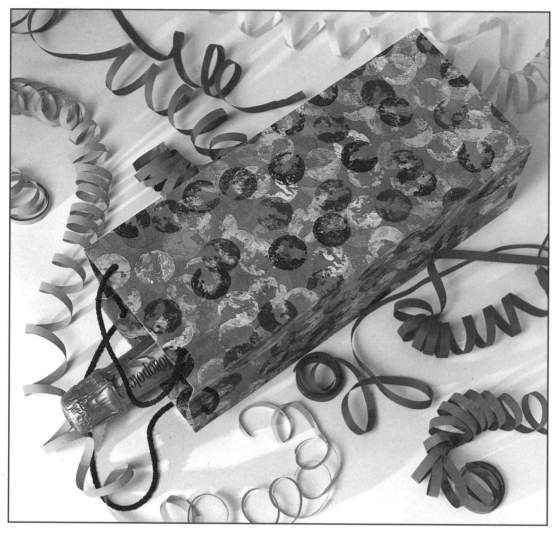

MATERIALS

To make the gift bag shown *below left* you will need:

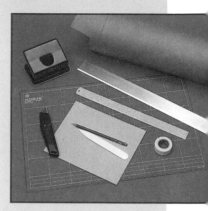

Above, A1 (33 x 23⅜in) sheet airforce blue manila paper; A5 (8¼ x 5⅞in) sheet of thin grey card; cutting mat; ruler; metal ruler; pencil; craft knife; bone folder; hole punch; 15mm (⅝in) wide double-sided adhesive tape.

Above, wine bottle cork; 1m (1yd) black lacing cord; newsprint; small paintbrush; sheet of glass; jam jar; acrylic paints in cadmium red light, emerald green, primrose yellow, cobalt, orange, black, white; acrylic retarder; all-purpose cloth.

Continuing our course in papercraft, we show you how to apply paper folding techniques to make a decorated gift bag for a bottle. The simple method of block printing the design with a cork wittily reflects the function of the bag.

Carrier bags have reached designer status today and are no longer regarded as disposable functional packaging. Shops and manufacturers are keen not only to advertise brand names, but to produce cult objects designed for re-use. This project shows you the techniques you will need to make your own individual designer gift bags.

Our bottle bag is constructed from manila paper which is available in a wide range of colours and weights. When you have scored all the fold lines, the decoration is applied before the bag is assembled. The paper structure is reinforced at the top and bottom with thin card to add strength at the stress points, and the design allows for the bag to be stored flat when not in use. The way the

cord is threaded allows for the opening of the bag to be drawn shut.

Measure out the dimensions of the bag accurately, and be patient when folding along the score lines to ensure that you get the best results. When you have understood how the structure works, you will be able to design your own bag with different dimensions to suit another purpose.

Cork stamp

For the decoration, which is stamped on to the paper with a cork, we have used acrylic paint, which is waterproof and fast-drying. To slow down the drying rate a little, dilute the paint with acrylic retarder rather than water, but do not add too much retarder as this will tend to thin the colour. Test the cover of the paint on a scrap of paper first.

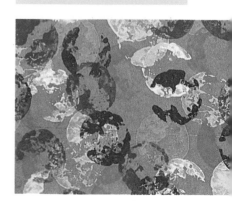

CUTTING DIAGRAM (all measurements in mm)

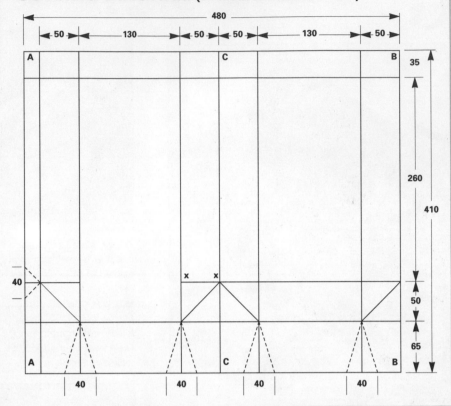

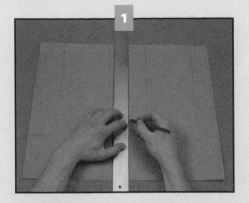

1 Cut the manila paper to 480 x 410mm (19 x 16⅛in) with the craft knife and ruler. Using the diagram as a guide, measure and draw all the lines with a pencil.

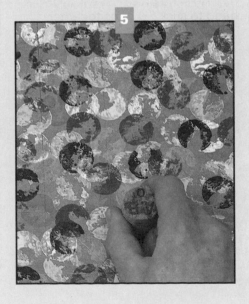

2 Score along all the solid lines with a bone folder against the straight edge. Cut along the dotted lines and remove the triangular sections.

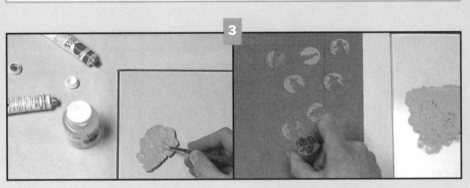

3 Cover the work surface with newsprint. Squeeze 1cm (½in) of white acrylic paint on to a sheet of glass and add a touch of cadmium red light and two drops of acrylic retarder. Mix with a paintbrush to make pink. Spread the paint evenly on the glass sheet with the paintbrush. Dab the end of the cork into the paint. Print randomly on the marked side of the manila paper, replenishing the colour on the cork after two prints. Blot the surface of the printed paper with newsprint to remove excess colour. Leave to dry for five minutes. Clean the glass, brush and cork with a wet cloth.

4 Repeat the printing process, following step 3, with the following colours: orange, emerald green, cobalt and primrose yellow, mixing each colour with white and leaving it to dry before printing the next.

5 Print with pure cadmium red light, then with pure black. Blot and leave to dry between each colour.

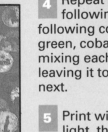

6 When completely dry, fold the paper on all the lengthwise scored lines and press down on the fold with the back of the hand to make a sharp crease as shown.

7 Crease the horizontal lines (except line X-X), then crease the lines of the central V inwards.

8 Carefully crease the line marked X-X on the diagram as shown.

9 Stick a strip of double-sided tape to the upper side of the flap A-A, trimming it flush with the ends.

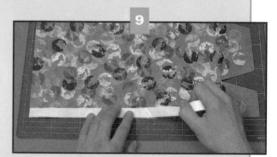

10 Turn the card over and cut the tape away from the triangular section.

11 Remove the backing paper from the tape. Match the edge of flap B-B with the score line of flap A-A and press flat with your hand to stick the flaps together.

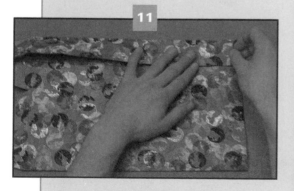

12 Fold in the top 35mm (1⅜in), then fold in at lines B-B and C-C. Punch two holes through all thicknesses at the top, as shown.

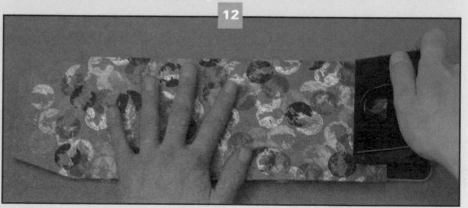

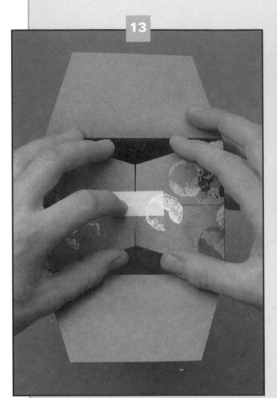

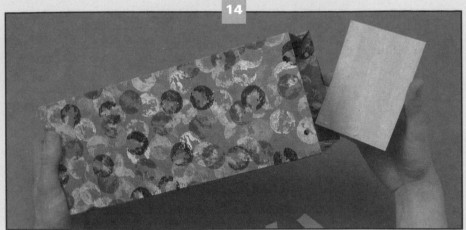

13 Cut a 3cm (1¼in) strip of double-sided tape and stick together the two smaller flaps of the base as shown. Peel the backing from the tape and stick down a large flap. Stick the two large flaps together with another 3cm (1¼in) strip of tape. Put your hand in the bag and press to stick firmly.

14 From the grey card, cut one piece 125 x 95mm (5 x 3¾in) and two pieces 125 x 30mm (5 x 1³⁄₁₆in). Cut 3 lengths of double-sided tape and stick to one side of the 125 x 95mm (5 x 3¾in) card. Peel the tape backing and stick the card to the inside base of the bag.

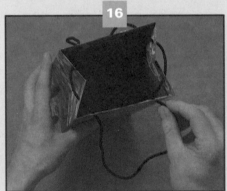

15 Punch holes centrally at one side of each 125 x 30mm (5 x 1³⁄₁₆in) piece of card and then trim a 2mm (¹⁄₁₆in) strip off this edge. Fit these under each long flap to check for fit. Stick double-sided tape on both sides of the card between the holes and peel off the backing paper. Fit inside the flaps, lining up the holes, and press firmly.

16 Thread the cord through the holes as shown, and tie the ends together inside the bag.

17 The bag is ready for use. If you want to store it flat, crease along the scored line as shown.

You can make a bag to your own colour scheme by using a different coloured paper or different coloured paints. A bright red cord would add a lively touch.

PAPERCRAFT

GIFT BOXES

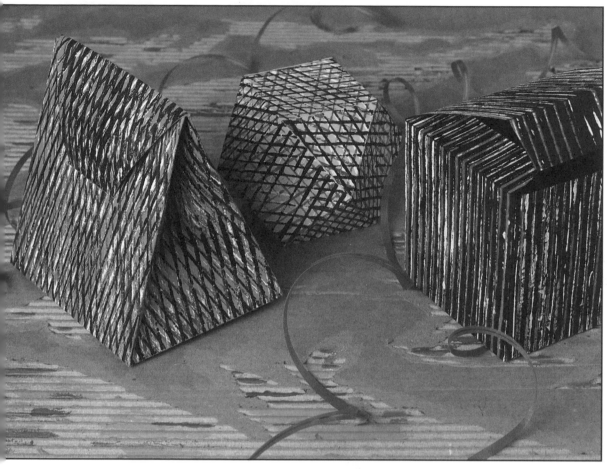

MATERIALS

To make the decorated gift boxes shown *below left* you will need:

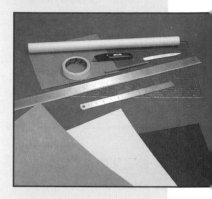

Above, 3 sheets of 300gsm (140lb) card, 500 x 350mm (20 x 14in), black, blue and yellow; cutting mat; craft knife; metal straight edge; ruler; bone folder; pencil; newsprint; medium grade sandpaper; double-sided adhesive tape.

Above, sheet of corrugated card or card cut from a corrugated cardboard box, 500 x 500mm (20 x 20in); Japanese barren; white emulsion paint; acrylic paints, cadmium red and Mars black; 6cm (2½in) decorator's brush; small paintbrush; palette or plate for mixing paints; jam jar.

In this papercraft project we show you how to make a range of gift boxes from sheets of coloured card printed with decorative patterns and folded to create geometric shapes, each with a different type of opening.

When you have a special gift for someone it can be frustrating if you cannot find entertaining and original packaging for it. We have devised a range of gift boxes that are easy to make and decorate, and because they are both durable and attractive they can be used again rather than simply thrown away.

Creating a net
The two-dimensional shape from which a carton or box is folded and glued is known as a 'net'. In this project we have designed nets for three different geometric shapes, ranging from a simple cube to a multi-faceted 'honeycomb' shape.

If your gift boxes are to have a professional looking finish it is important to be very accurate when measuring, drawing, scoring and cutting the net. All the folds should be sharp and clean, and the flaps on the box lids should slide into place with just the right amount of friction to prevent

them from sliding or springing open.

In order to make crisp, accurate folds in the card, the surface must first be scored with the sharp end of a bone folder. Scoring compresses the fibres in the card, creating an indentation along the score line, and a ridge on the reverse side. The card can then be folded precisely along the scored line without it breaking up into a ragged edge. The card is folded with the indentation on the outside and the ridge on the inside for minimum stretch; if the ridge is on the outside the surface is stretched taut and may break up along the fold.

Printed lines
The colourful printed decoration on our boxes makes ingenious use of ordinary corrugated cardboard. The multi-linear patterns are printed by laying the cut-out box 'net' at various angles on the painted surface of a sheet of corrugated card and burnishing to transfer the paint to the net.

KEY TO THE DIAGRAMS

▬	double-sided tape
▬	cut away these areas
– – – –	fold line
———	cut line

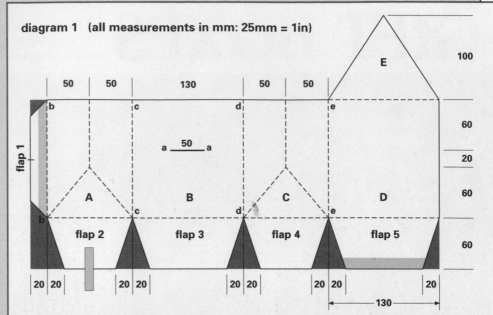

diagram 1 (all measurements in mm: 25mm = 1in)

1 Using diagram **1** as a guide, measure out and draw all the lines accurately with pencil on the blue sheet of card. Using a craft knife and metal straight edge, cut out the 'net' (the card shape) and cut the slot aa on face B. With the pointed end of the bone folder held against the metal straight edge, score along all the dotted lines.

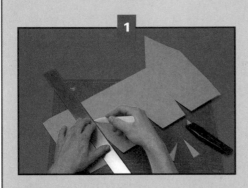

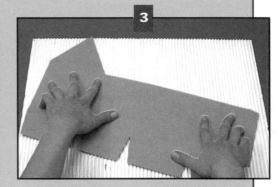

2 If you are using corrugated cardboard cut from a box, strip off the covering layer of paper to reveal the corrugations. Remove any flecks of paper from the grooves by rubbing with the folded edge of a sheet of sandpaper.

3 With the decorator's brush, apply a coat of white emulsion paint to the surface of the corrugated card to seal it. Leave to dry for 20 minutes. Apply a second coat of paint and, while this is still wet, position the net on it, scored side down, at an angle of 60° to the vertical run of the corrugations. Lay a sheet of newsprint over the net and rub gently with the barren to transfer the paint to it. Remove the newsprint and discard it.

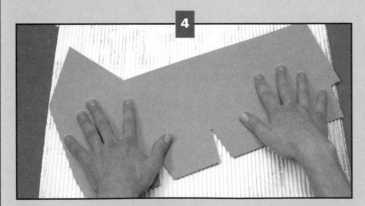

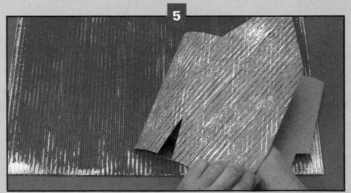

4 Peel the printed net away from the corrugated card and place to one side while you apply a further coat of white emulsion to the corrugated card. Replace the net at the opposite angle to that in step 3 and burnish again using the barren and a fresh sheet of newsprint. Peel away the net, which will now be printed with a diamond pattern.

5 Squeeze about 10cm (4in) of cadmium red acrylic paint onto a palette and dilute with water to a thick, creamy consistency. Apply this to the corrugated card — the white underlayer will lighten the tone of the red slightly. Position the net at almost the same angle as in step 3, so that the red lines are slightly out of register with the white ones. Print as before, and set aside.

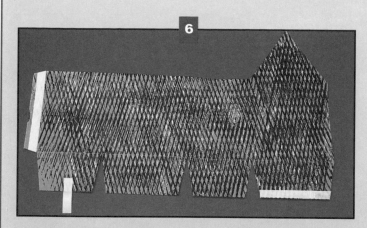

6 Re-coat the corrugated card with red paint and print on to the net, placing it at the opposite angle to that in step 5. Repeat the painting and printing process with the black paint, again placing the net so that the black lines are slightly out of register with the red and white lines. Attach a 15mm (⅝in)-wide strip of double-sided adhesive tape to flaps 1 and 5, on the printed side, as shown, and a 55mm (2⅛in)-length to flap 2, as shown.

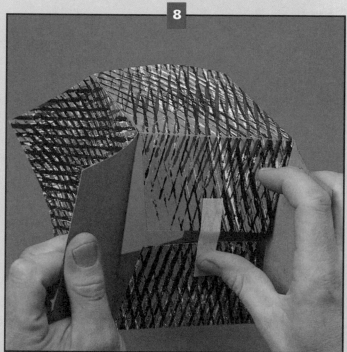

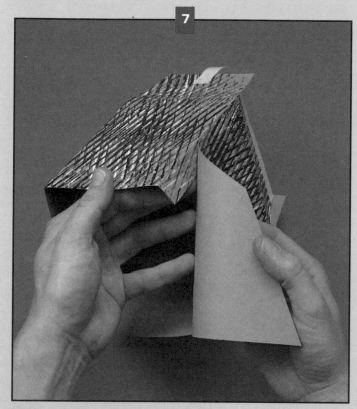

7 Fold along the score lines bb, cc, dd and ee. Remove the backing strip from the tape on flap 1 and form the box by sticking the tape to the edge of back section D.

8 Stick flaps 2 and 4 together as shown. Then remove the backing strip from the tape on flap 2.

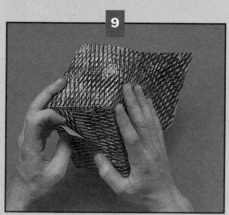

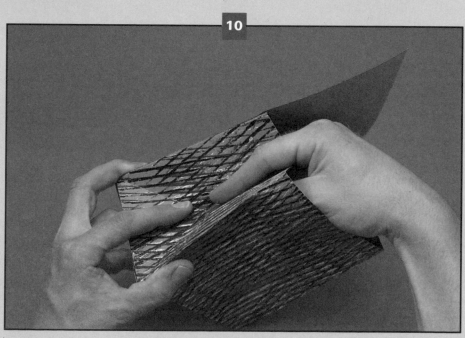

9 Remove the backing strip from the tape on flap 5 and stick flap 3 over flap 5 as shown.

10 Gently bend the sides of the box inwards along the Y-shaped score lines.

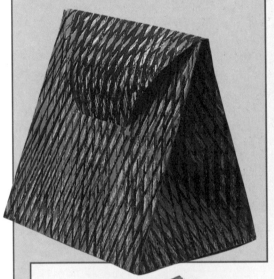

11 Cut out a piece of card 128 x 98mm (5 x 4in) and stick it to the inside base of the box to strengthen it. Finally, close the box by inserting the pointed end of section E into the slot on face B.

ALTERNATIVE SHAPES

To make the square box, draw up diagram **2** on the sheet of black card. Cut out and score along all the dotted lines. Print the net as described above, this time using the corrugated card to make a pattern of vertical stripes. Apply double-sided tape where indicated on the diagram, remove the backing strip and form the box as shown.

To make the many-faceted box, draw up diagram **3** on the sheet of yellow card. Cut out the net, score and print it in the same way as you did for the first box, rotating the net at each printing to create a diamond pattern. Fold up and glue the tabs (with double-sided tape) as shown, always joining a triangle to a square.

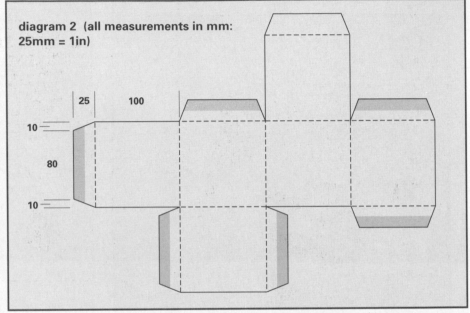

diagram 2 (all measurements in mm: 25mm = 1in)

25   100
10
80
10

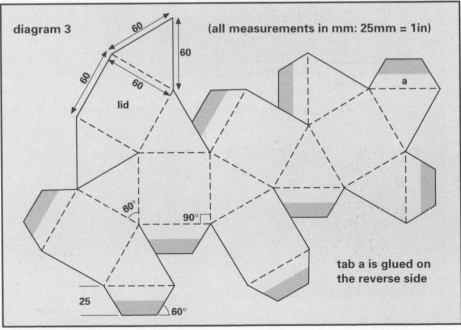

diagram 3   (all measurements in mm: 25mm = 1in)

60
60
60
60
lid
a
80°
90°
tab a is glued on the reverse side
25
60°

Get into the habit of taking apart unusual shaped boxes that come your way, so that you can see how they are constructed. Ideas for new shapes can be gleaned from architectural and other man-made constructions.

PAPERCRAFT

ART PORTFOLIO

MATERIALS

To make the portfolio shown *below left* you will need:

Above, cutting mat; sheet of 1.96mm (¹⁄₁₆in) thick greyboard; piece of black library buckram, 500 x 500mm (20 x 20in); piece of royal blue library buckram, 500 x 500mm (20 x 20in); A1 (33 x 23³⁄₈in) sheet of black manilla card; PVA (white) glue; bone folder; craft knife; metal straight edge; ruler; 5cm (2in) decorator's brush; newsprint; pencil.

Above, 2m (2yd) of 12mm (¹⁄₂in) black hem ribbon; 12mm (¹⁄₂in) chisel; hammer; scrap wood; acrylic paint, orange and black; pair of dividers; masking tape; 2 small pieces of thin card; sheet of glass; set square.

This stylish artist's portfolio has a concertina spine and hand-decorated covers. The project uses some of the bookbinding techniques you learned when making the stationery box, and introduces you to some new skills.

Victorian architects and print collectors might have been seen carrying a portfolio very similar to ours. A Victorian portfolio might have been covered with book cloth or with buckram (which has a washable surface), or with leather or marbled papers, which were fashionable at the time; occasionally they were covered with vellum (calfskin).

Going with the grain

When cutting out the board it is important that the grain runs in the right direction. Test the board for the direction of the grain (see Stationery Box). Cut the pieces so that the grain runs along the length of the boards, giving the longer edge greater resistance with some flexibility on the short edge. You will notice that the greyboard will start to bend along the short edge when you glue on the buckram covers, but this will be counteracted when the paper is glued to the inside of the boards, and any further warping should be eradicated if the finished portfolio is pressed under a heavy weight.

It is important that you cut the pieces as you need them. Use the measurements we have given for the board and the black buckram, but be sure to check the measurements for the blue buckram and manilla card with your own project as there might be slight variations according to the accuracy of your work. If you choose a thinner paper to cover the boards it may stretch once it is glued. If this happens, trim it to size with a sharp knife.

HELPFUL HINT

Bookbinding materials and tools may be available in your local craft shop, but if you have trouble obtaining them locally, you can buy the materials mail order. Ask your craft centre, library, or antiquarian book shop for the address of a mail order supplier.

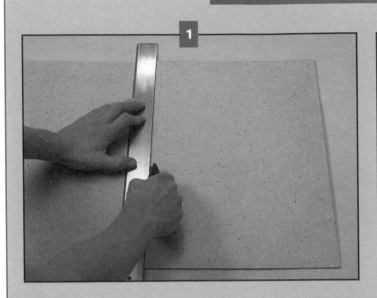

Diagram 1   Cut from greyboard (all measurements in mm)

420

spine template

grain direction

42   297   62   35   42

25mm = 1in

1 Mark up and cut the greyboard with the grain running along the length of the pieces. Cut two pieces 420 x 297mm (16½ x 11¾in), using a sharp craft knife and the metal straight edge. With a pencil, mark out on each piece a line 42mm (1⅝in) from the edge of one long side. On the opposite long side of one piece, mark a line 62mm (2½in) from the edge. Cut a strip of board 420 x 35mm (16½ x 1⅜in) to act as a template to space the spine. (See diagram **1** *above right*.)

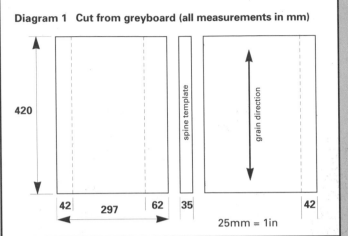

2 Mark and cut the black buckram on the wrong side of the fabric with a sharp craft knife. Cut one strip, **a**, 160 x 480mm (6¼ x 19in) to form the spine of the folder; 2 strips, **b**, 70 x 480mm (2¾ x 19in) to cover the outer edges of the boards; one strip, **c**, 410 x 60mm (16 x 2⅜in) to reinforce the spine. (See diagram **2** *left*.)

Diagram 2   Cut from black buckram (measurements in mm)

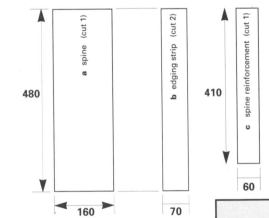

a spine (cut 1)

b edging strip (cut 2)

c spine reinforcement (cut 1)

480

410

160   70   60

25mm = 1in

3 Cover the table with newsprint and, using the decorator's brush, stipple PVA (white) glue evenly on the reverse of the strip of buckram for the spine, **a**. Discard the sheet of newsprint, pick up the strip at top and bottom and line up one edge of the buckram on the 62mm (2½in) line drawn on one of the boards (this leaves 30mm (1³⁄₁₆in) overlapping at the top and bottom of the board). Rub down gently with the side of your hand, then turn the board and buckram over. Working quickly, place the spine template next to the board and place the other board in position, making sure that all three pieces are square to one another (check with the metal straight edge).

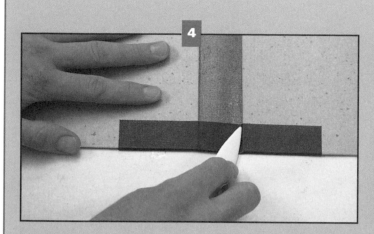

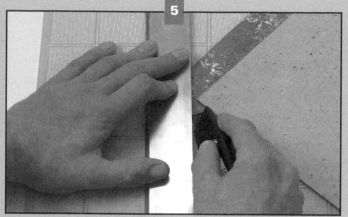

4 Flip the boards over and rub down the buckram. Turn the boards over again and remove the template from the spine. Fold the edges of buckram over on to the board and press them down firmly with the bone folder. Glue strip **c** on the inside of the spine and press down firmly (this will reinforce the spine and covers the join with a 10mm overlap on both boards).

5 Cover one of the edging strips **b** with glue and line up one edge with the 42mm (1⅝in) pencil line on one board (leaving a 30mm (1³⁄₁₆in) overlap top and bottom). Rub down and turn the boards over. Cut the buckram at an angle of 45º at the corners, 2mm (¹⁄₁₆in) from the corner of the board.

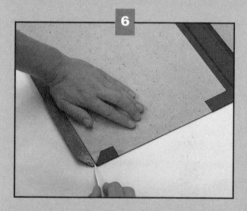

6 Press the short edge down on the inside of the board and then neaten the corner with the point of the bone folder. Repeat for the other end. Stick down the long edge. Glue the second edging strip on the other board in the same way, following steps 5 and 6.

7 Cut 2 pieces of blue buckram to fit the area of the boards on the outside of the folder between the black buckram with an overlap of 5mm (³⁄₁₆in) on both sides (480 x 200mm; 19 x 7⅞in). Mark this 5mm (³⁄₁₆in) point on one strip of black buckram on each board for positioning. Glue up one piece of blue buckram and line up with the marks. Rub down with your hand, turn over and press down the edges on the inside. Turn over again and rub down firmly with a bone folder, protecting the cloth with a sheet of newsprint. Glue the blue buckram on the other board in the same way.

8 To form the concertina spine, fold the buckram inwards and use the bone folder to sharpen the point of the fold. Press the spine with your hands then carefully open out the folder and rub down the fold with the bone folder to create a sharp crease. You may need to press the spine in its closed position under a weight for 10 minutes to allow it to dry flat.

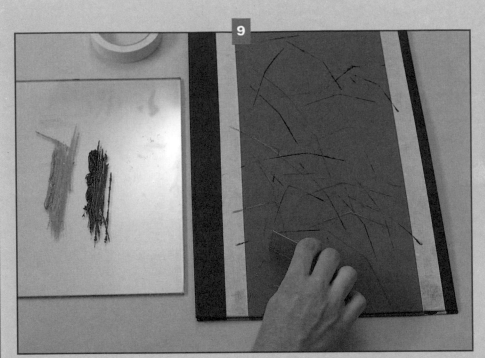

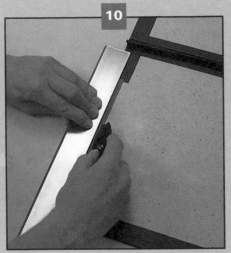

10 On the inside of the folder use dividers to measure 10mm (⅜in) from the edge all the way around on the turnovers. Cut off the surplus buckram to leave an even border.

9 Mask off the edge of the black buckram with masking tape. Squeeze out some orange and black acrylic paint on to a sheet of glass. Dab the edge of a small piece of card into the paint and dab the colours randomly on to the blue buckram until the whole area is patterned with interesting marks (bend the card if you like). Leave to dry for at least one hour. Remove the masking tape. Turn the portfolio over and repeat.

MARKING THE HOLES

Mark the centre point of all four short sides and, 20mm (¾in) from the outer edge, mark off a 12mm (½in) line with pencil, centred on the mark. On the long edges measure 100mm (4in) from each corner, 20mm (¾in) from the edge of the board, and mark off a 12mm (½in) line from this point as shown.

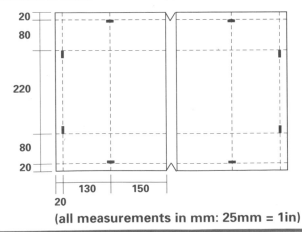

(all measurements in mm: 25mm = 1in)

11 Open out the folder and mark the position of the holes for the ribbon as shown *above*. Place a block of wood underneath one of the marks and punch a hole through with a hammer and 12mm (½in) chisel held vertically. Repeat for all the marks.

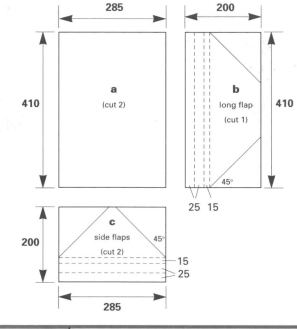

CUTTING THE MANILLA CARD

Cut out the black manilla card as shown in the diagram, with the grain running down the length of the pieces (if necessary, adapt the measurements to suit your own folder). You will need: **a** two pieces. These are needed to cover the inside of the boards to within 5mm (³⁄₁₆in) of the inside edge of the folder; **b** one piece (for the long side); **c** two pieces (for the short sides).

(all measurements in mm: 25mm = 1in)

285

a
(cut 2)

410

200

b
long flap
(cut 1)

410

45°

25 15

200

c
side flaps
(cut 2)

45°

15

25

285

12 Cut the ribbon into eight 20cm (8in) lengths, and feed them through the holes from the outside leaving 30mm (1in) on the inside boards. Glue and press down. Leave to dry for 20 minutes.

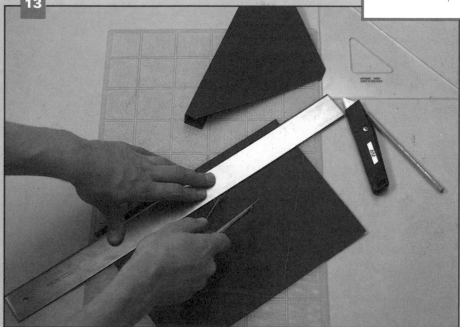

13 Cut out the black manilla card, following the instructions *top right*. On all three flaps, measure 25mm (1in) from the long edges and score the paper with the point of the dividers. Measure off another 25mm (1in) and score the paper again. At both ends of all the flaps, mark a point 15mm (⁵⁄₈in) from this line and draw a line with a 45° set square. Cut along these diagonal lines with a sharp knife. Fold along the scored lines with the cut on the outside of the folds.

14 Glue one of the large pieces, **a**, to the inside of one of the boards. Attach each side flap, **c**, to the other board by glueing the scored side of the first 25mm (1in) fold and sticking in place, with the scoreline 3mm (⅛in) from the edge of the folder. Make sure that it is square to all edges; press down.

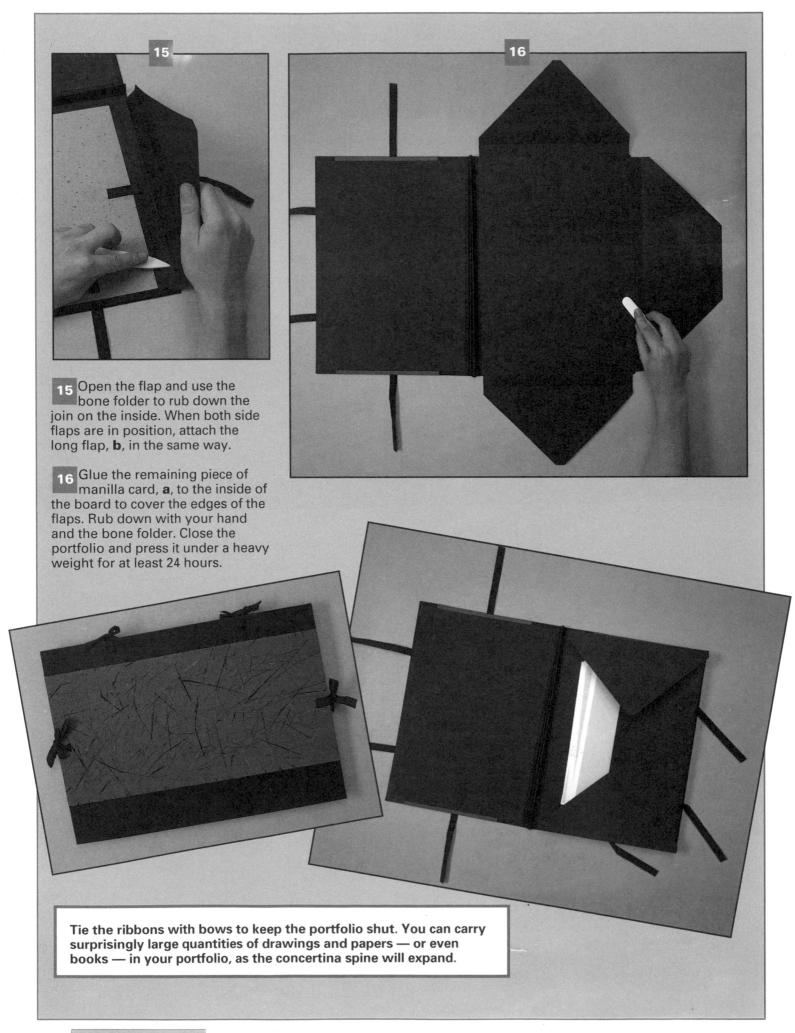

15 Open the flap and use the bone folder to rub down the join on the inside. When both side flaps are in position, attach the long flap, **b**, in the same way.

16 Glue the remaining piece of manilla card, **a**, to the inside of the board to cover the edges of the flaps. Rub down with your hand and the bone folder. Close the portfolio and press it under a heavy weight for at least 24 hours.

Tie the ribbons with bows to keep the portfolio shut. You can carry surprisingly large quantities of drawings and papers — or even books — in your portfolio, as the concertina spine will expand.

PAPERCRAFT

DECORATED TRAY

Above, eight sheets of origami or craft paper in various colours, including one sheet of purple paper at least 340 x 245cm (13½ x 10in) for the background; five sheets of A3 (16½ x 11¹¹/₁₆in) sugar paper; plastic tray, 340 x 245cm (13½ x 10in), for the mould; large plastic tray or piece of wood to protect working surface; PVA (white) glue; bowl; scissors; petroleum jelly.

Above, piece of fine sandpaper; soft rag; polyurethane varnish; artist's nylon-bristle paintbrush, size 14; varnish brush; nylon-bristle paste brush, 25mm (1in) wide; small palette; artist's acrylic paint, ivory black and dark blue; scalpel.

Papier-mâché is an old craft that is currently enjoying a revival of interest. The techniques are simple and the materials inexpensive, yet you can produce fascinating results — from works of art to humble puppets. This decorated tray makes a suitable first project, as it introduces the technique of layering paper.

Layering, or laminating, paper is one of the most commonly used techniques for making papier-mâché objects. It involves building up many layers of glue-soaked paper; this is a simple process, but one that must be done with great care to ensure a good finish. The technique has many applications and is well worth experimenting with, although it is best to start by casting from a simple object such as a bowl or, as in this case, a small rectangular tray. You can use a slightly larger tray if you wish, adapting the design to fit, but the tray should not be too large, otherwise the papier-mâché may warp while drying.

The design used here was inspired by Matisse papercuts and the individual pieces are cut from good quality coloured paper. You can use your own design, but for a first attempt it is best to restrict your range of colours and shapes.

USING THE TEMPLATES

The template shows all the elements you will need to duplicate the decorated tray design. Each shape must be traced and cut out separately. For example, you will need to trace three individual shapes for the pattern in the top left-hand corner: the acorn leaf, the rib of the leaf and the square. When you have traced and cut all the patterns you should have 42 shapes.

1 Enlarge the template on a photocopier to 200%. Trace the designs on to tracing paper and separate each shape by cutting loosely around it. Put one of the tracings on a piece of coloured paper and use the tracing as a guide to cut out the shape. Continue until you have all the cut-outs you require.

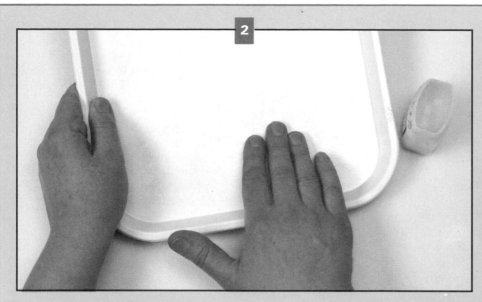

2 Using your fingers, coat the top and inner edges of the tray that you are using for your mould with petroleum jelly. This will prevent the first layer of paper sticking to the mould. Spread the jelly evenly over the surface.

3 Fold each sheet of sugar paper into four and tear into pieces along the fold lines. (See Tearing and Pasting box.) Paste the torn paper on both sides; the glue must be allowed to soak through the paper to render it more flexible, but it should be damp, not wet, or it will stretch unevenly and create ripples when it dries.

TEARING AND PASTING

Always fold and tear the paper along the grain. You can find out which way the grain runs on your paper by tearing a piece first lengthwise and then crosswise — the grain will be immediately obvious simply because the paper tears more easily along it.

You can use cellulose (wallpaper) paste instead of PVA (white) glue but this takes longer to dry. If you are using PVA (white) glue you must first dilute it with enough water to give it the consistency of single cream. The mixture is sticky to work with, but it gives added strength to the finished tray.

4 Lay the pieces of paper on to the mould one at a time, gently smoothing each one out to make sure that any air bubbles are released — these can become trapped between the layers of paper and disfigure the completed piece. Continue to apply the paper, overlapping each piece. Gradually build up the layers, using larger pieces in the centre of the tray. Use straight-edged pieces along the edges of the tray.

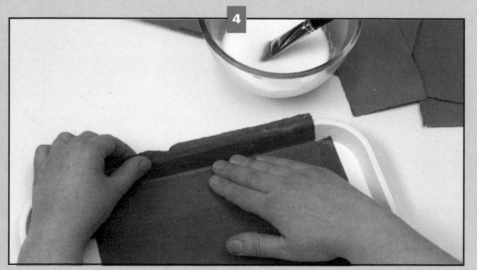

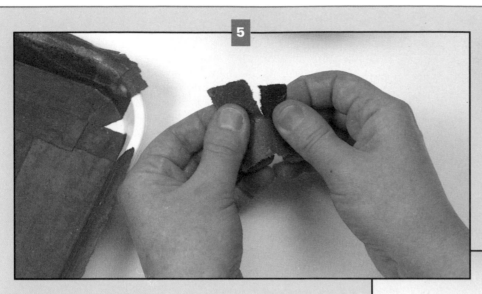

5 To layer the curved corners, take a piece of pasted sugar paper and tear it into small strips.

6 Lay the strips vertically around the curve, working from left to right and overlapping each one. Continue to lay down paper on the bottom and rim until you have completed 10 layers. Allow to dry overnight.

7 Place the purple sheet of paper you are using for the background on the tray and mould it carefully into the shape of the tray so that it creases around the edges. Remove the paper and use the creases as a guide to cut the paper to the shape of the bottom of the tray.

8 Coat the top and underside of the paper with glue and place it on the tray. Smooth the paper carefully by pressing it with the flat of your hand to release any air bubbles.

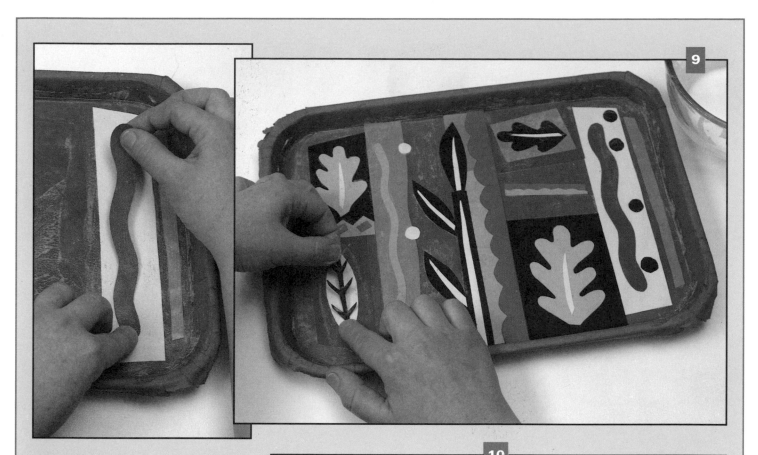

9 Arrange the coloured cut-outs on the table in their right positions. Working from right to left across the tray, glue down all the coloured cut-outs. Coat with another layer of glue. The glue always appears milky when wet but it will dry to a clear finish. Smooth with the fingers if any bubbles or ripples appear.

10 Allow the tray to dry thoroughly at an even temperature — an airing cupboard is ideal. When it is dry, use a scalpel to trim the uneven and overlapping rim of the paper-layered tray flush with the rim of the mould.

11 Lift the paper cast from the mould and lightly sand the cut edge to make it smooth and even.

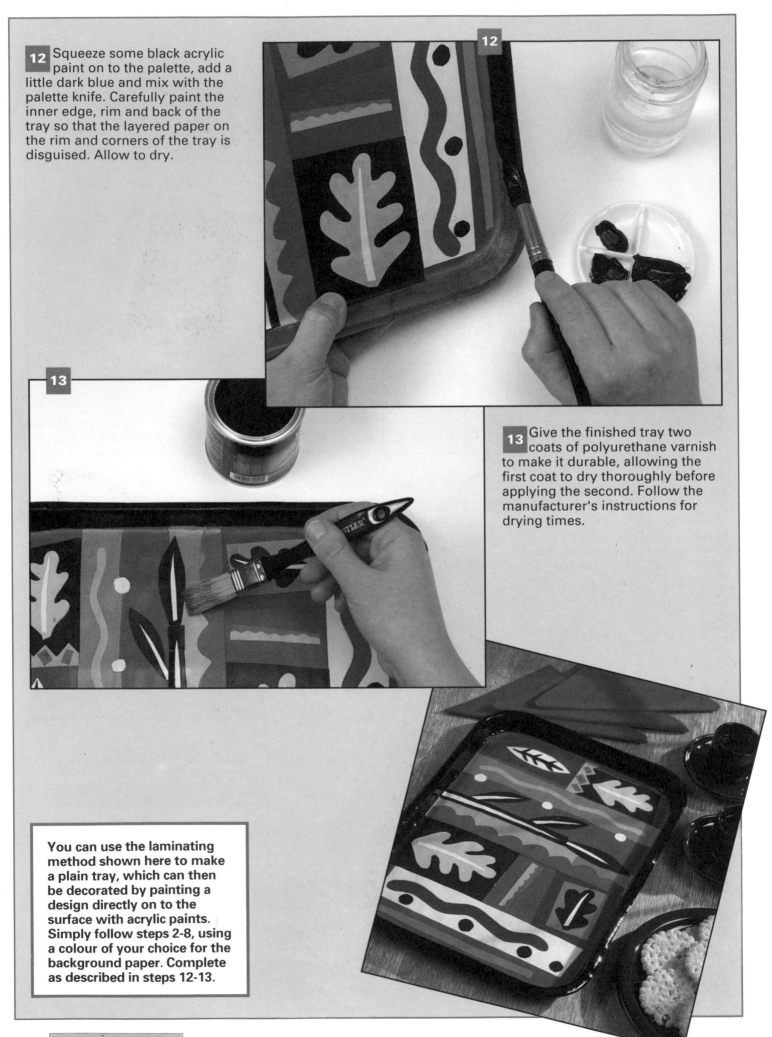

12 Squeeze some black acrylic paint on to the palette, add a little dark blue and mix with the palette knife. Carefully paint the inner edge, rim and back of the tray so that the layered paper on the rim and corners of the tray is disguised. Allow to dry.

13 Give the finished tray two coats of polyurethane varnish to make it durable, allowing the first coat to dry thoroughly before applying the second. Follow the manufacturer's instructions for drying times.

You can use the laminating method shown here to make a plain tray, which can then be decorated by painting a design directly on to the surface with acrylic paints. Simply follow steps 2-8, using a colour of your choice for the background paper. Complete as described in steps 12-13.

PAPERCRAFT

MEXICAN SUN MASK

MATERIALS

To make the sun mask shown *below left* you will need:

Above, 2kg (4½lb) plasticine; one packet wall paper paste (cold water paste powder, not cellulose paste); PVA glue; wooden board at least 50 x 35cm (20 x 14 in) ; scalpel; jam jar or bowl; two newspapers, of different colours if possible.

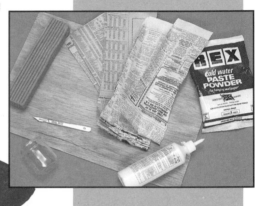

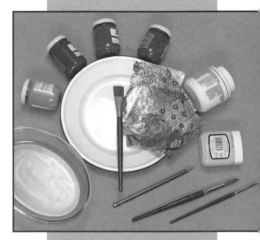

Masks have a long history, going back to ancient Egypt and ancient Greece. Our colourful Mexican sun mask is inspired by ritual masks used in carnivals and is made from papier mâché which is easy to mould and light to wear.

You can find wonderful and varied examples of papier mâché masks from such diverse cultures as Japan, India, Switzerland and Mexico. The masks are usually painted very brightly and have the ability to disguise and transform the character of the wearer; they have therefore been used throughout history for carnivals and ritual ceremonies.

The features of the face are very powerful symbols to work with, and there are endless possibilities for creating character in your mask, from the most benign to the most demonic. It is well worth looking at examples of masks in museums for inspiration.

The design we have used was inspired by a Mexican sun mask. Bits of glittery paper from sweet wrappers have been used to enhance the original design, and the mask is painted in four bold colours to make a very striking image.

Above, acrylic gesso; sharp pencil; nylon artist's brushes, size 14 and 7 round and 20mm (3/4in) flat; petroleum jelly; Le Franc & Bourgeoise Flash acrylic paints in cobalt blue, orange, gold yellow and Tyrian rose; dish or palette, for mixing paints; bowl; foil sweet wrappers.

THE TEMPLATE

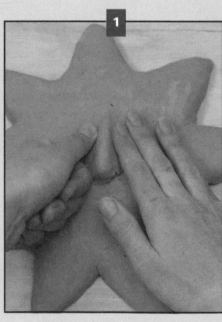

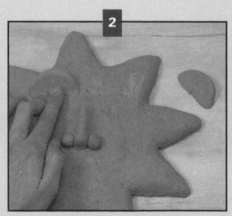

1 Photocopy the template at 166%. Cut out the shape, place it on the wooden board and draw around it with a pencil. Remove the template and smear petroleum jelly over the board inside the pencil line. Put the plasticine in the centre of the shape, setting aside a handful to use for the features. Form the large lump of plasticine into a star shape with your hands. The plasticine should be about 25mm (1in) thick in the centre and about 10mm (½in) thick at the points of the star. To form the nose, take a small piece of plasticine and roll it into a sausage shape. Place it on the 'face' and mould it into shape.

2 Roll out two small round shapes and apply one either side of the nose to make the nostrils. Make two 'lemon wedge' shapes for the eyebrows and two round shapes for the eyes.

3 Put two small round shapes on top of the eyes to make the pupils. Roll two lengths of plasticine into thin sausages and coil up loosely. Put one either side of the nose for the cheeks.

4 For the mouth, roll out another sausage shape and join the ends together. Form into a rounded heart shape and apply to the face. Smear petroleum jelly all over the completed mould.

5 To prepare the glue paste, mix one cup of water with one tablespoon PVA (white) glue and add one heaped tablespoon of wallpaper paste. Mix together to a consistency of thick cream. Tear the newspapers into small pieces, approximately 20 x 10mm (1 x ½in) Smear both sides of a piece of paper with the paste and stick it down on the mould. Continue until the mould is completely covered.

6 Gradually build up eight layers of glue-soaked newspaper, using alternate colours of paper (eg, pink and white) to help you count the layers you have done. Allow the papier mâché to dry thoroughly for about two or three days at an even temperature (an airing cupboard is ideal).

7 Carefully prise the mask from the mould, beginning with the points of the star.

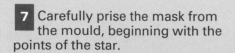

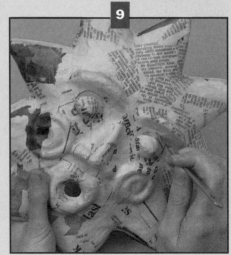

8 Trim the edges of the mask with a scalpel or a pair of scissors.

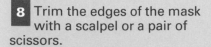

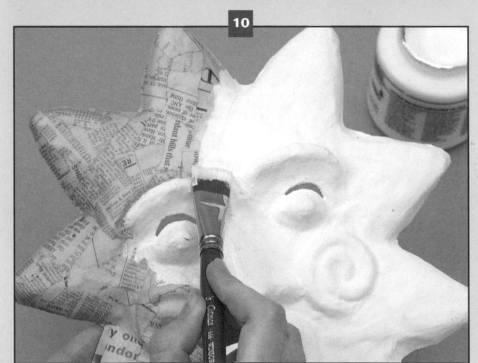

9 Using the scalpel, cut a circle in the centre of the mouth. Draw a small crescent-moon shape above each eyeball and cut these out with a scalpel.

10 Paint the mask with acrylic gesso, using a 20mm (¾in) flat brush. Leave to dry for 15 to 30 minutes and then apply another two coats, leaving to dry between applications.

11 Using the larger round brush, paint the back of the mask with the cobalt blue, adding a little water to the paint if it is too thick. On the front, draw a circle to separate the face from the points of the 'star'. Paint the 'star' pink (you can give it two coats if you wish).

12 Paint the face yellow, leaving the eyebrows, eyes and mouth white.

13 Using the small round brush and the cobalt blue, paint in the pupils. Draw some diagonal stripes on the eyebrows and fill in the rest of the eyebrows with blue paint, as shown.

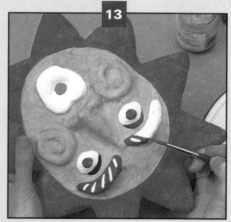

14 Draw small white dots on the mouth with a pencil and paint around them with blue to fill in the rest of the mouth. Paint the spirals on the cheeks orange.

15 Smooth out your pieces of coloured foil and cut into roughly-shaped 'squares'. Cut smaller pieces to place in the centre of the larger ones. Stick the pieces down with glue on the points of the star.

16 Cut out some narrow strips of foil, slightly on the curve, and stick them down around the edge of the face, as shown.

To enable you to wear your mask, crescent-shaped holes are cut above the eyes and a hole is cut in the centre of the mouth to allow you to breathe! To secure the mask when wearing it, make a small hole with a hole punch either side of the mask and tie a length of shearing elastic to these holes to fit your head.

Alternatively, you may just want to display your mask; you could make a series of different masks from different cultures to create a stunning wall display.

LAMP BASE

In this project we show you how to make the papier-mâché lamp base to team up with the paper lampshade featured earlier — so completing the 'Old woman who lived in a shoe' nursery rhyme lamp for a child's room.

In the Decorated Tray project, a ready-made mould — a tray — was used to form the object, while in the Mexican Sun Mask project, you made a mould from plasticine. Here we show you how to make a simple mould using an empty mineral water bottle (although any round, plastic bottle of 1.5 litre (2¾ pint) capacity would do), which is then 'filled out' with plasticine to achieve the desired shape. This technique provides an excellent example of how it is possible to achieve a wide variety of shapes with papier-mâché. When you have completed the lamp base you should have enough confidence to experiment with other shapes, using various similar, or even different, materials to make other objects.

If you made the paper lampshade that goes with the base, you will probably already have the bayonet lamp fitting required for your lamp base. With the exception of the paints, the other materials are both inexpensive and readily available.

When you have completed your lamp base, we suggest that you spray it with a fire retardant such as Flambar. If you would like to give the base a glossier finish, you can then paint it with a fire retardant lacquer such as Poliac, following the manufacturer's instructions. Ask in your local art or craft shop for advice on selecting and using fire retardant products.

MATERIALS

To make the lamp base shown *below left* you will need:

Above, pencil; 150g (6oz) plasticine; packet of wallpaper paste; piece of board for working on; two newspapers, in different colours; 1.5 litre (2¾ pint) plastic bottle (such as a mineral water bottle); scalpel; large jam jar; scissors; petroleum jelly.

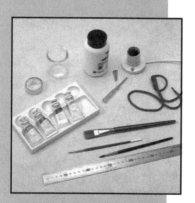

Above, acrylic gesso; three paint brushes, fine, medium and thick; designers gouache in red, green, blue and yellow; sticking tape, such as sellotape; steel ruler; one red boot lace; bayonet light fitting with screws and flex; small screwdriver; jam jar; steel ruler.

1 Using a pair of scissors or a scalpel, cut the plastic bottle into two sections, cutting about 250mm (10in) from the bottom. On the bottom section, cut out a semi-circle approximately 40mm (1½in) in depth and approximately two-thirds of the circumference. This will form the ankle of the boot.

2 Cut the neck off the top section and then cut it in half vertically.

Use one half to form the foot of the boot.

3 To assemble the mould, slot the ankle section over the end of the foot section, as shown, and stick it at the sides with sellotape or masking tape.

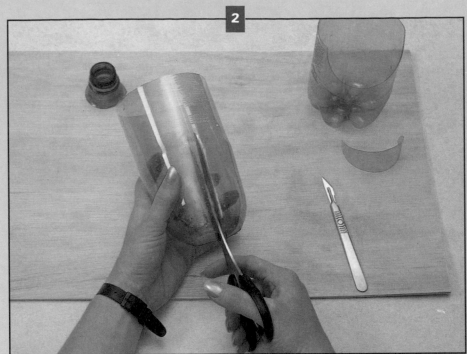

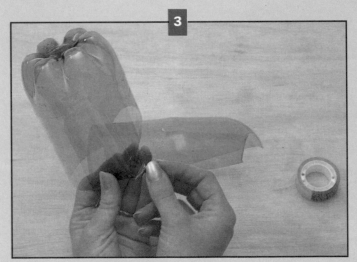

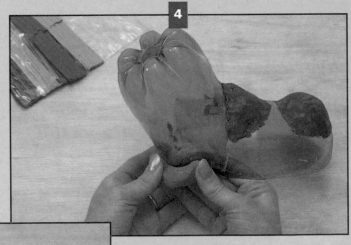

4 Knead the plasticine and divide it into three round pieces. Take one piece and mould it on to the toe of the boot. Pinch out the second piece so it is more sausage-shaped and place it over the join where the two sections of bottle meet. Use the third piece to mould the heel, smoothing out the plasticine as you work.

5 Cover the whole of your mould with petroleum jelly, applying it quite thickly.

6 To prepare the glue, fill the jam jar with water and add three heaped teaspoonfuls of wallpaper paste. Stir and leave for three minutes. Tear the newspapers into small pieces, approximately 20 x 10mm (1 x ½in). Stand the mould on the board, and with a brush, smear both sides of the pieces of paper with paste and stick them down on the mould until it is covered (apart from the 'sole'). Gradually build up six layers of paste-soaked newspaper using alternate colours of paper to help you count the completed layers. Leave the papier-mâché to dry for two days at an even temperature.

7 Carefully prise the boot from the mould and trim the edges with scissors.

8 To make the 'tongue', pencil in two parallel lines down the front of the ankle section. Using the scalpel, pierce the bottom of one of the lines and cut up this line, across the top and down the opposite line. Carefully bend the cut section forwards.

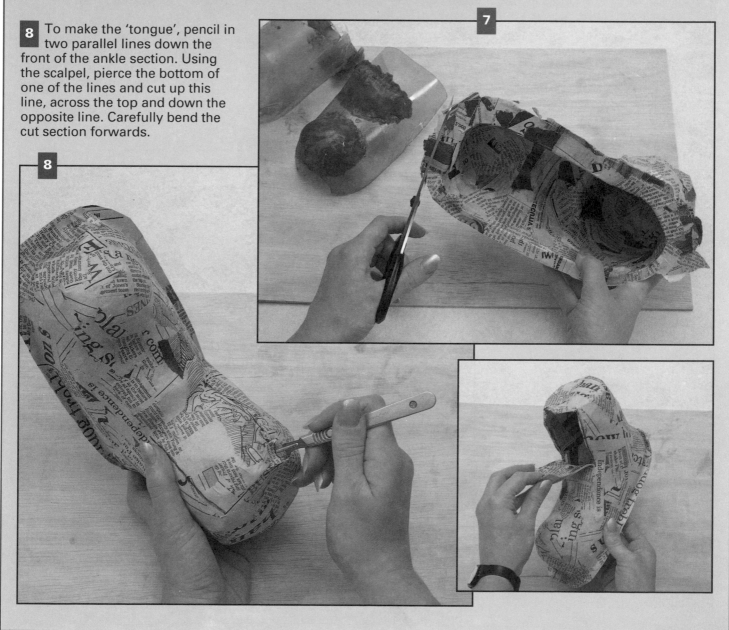

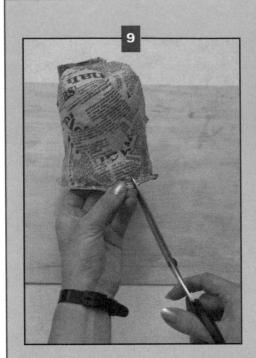

9 Cut out a small rectangle at the base of the heel for the light flex.

10 Build up two more layers of newspaper over the boot, covering the cut edges of the tongue and base. Leave to dry thoroughly.

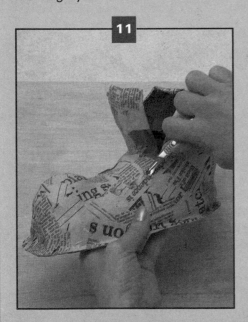

11 To make the holes for the laces, use the scalpel to pierce four holes opposite each other on either side of the foot, as shown.

12 Mix some acrylic gesso with a little yellow and red gouache to give a cream colour. Paint the boot inside and out with this, using the large paintbrush. Leave to dry for 15 to 30 minutes.

THE TEMPLATES

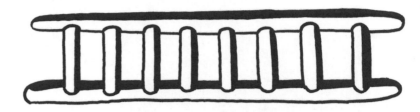

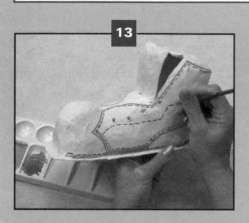

13 Mix up some red, blue and yellow gouache to make a light brown colour and, with a fine brush, use this to paint in the fine brown lines on the boot. With the fine brush and some red gouache, paint in the lines of red stitching.

14 Mix a pale green by tinting the gesso with green gouache. Paint the grass and ferns growing around and up the boot freehand. The fern effect can be achieved by filling the brush with paint and gently curving it around, then lifting it off to form a leaf. Using the ladder template as a guide, paint the ladder on the right side of the boot with some brown. Darken the brown a little and use this to paint in some 'shadows' on the edges of the rungs and the sides of the ladder.

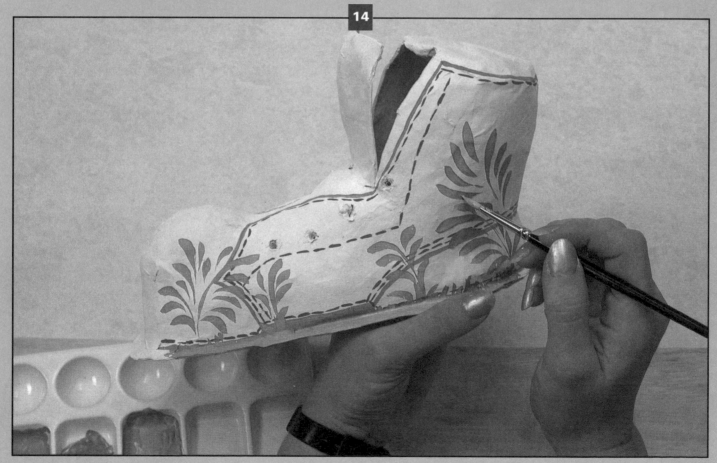

15 Paint brown around the lace holes. Put a small white highlight on the edge of each one. Using the window template as a guide, draw the windows on the toe and the back of the ankle and paint them with the acrylic gesso tinted pale blue. Mix red, green and blue with gesso to make pale grey and paint circular lines on the panes of glass.

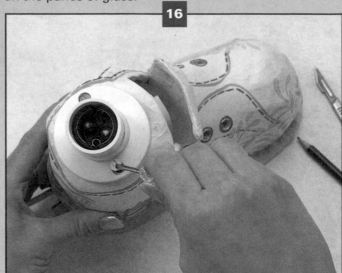

16 To attach the light fitting and flex, place the fitting on the top of the boot and, with a pencil, mark through the two screw holes. Remove the fitting and pierce the surface of the papier-mâché with the scalpel where you made your pencil marks. Make another hole in the centre of the top. Thread the flex through the centre hole, down into the boot and out through the rectangular hole in the heel. Screw the screws through the holes in the light fitting and the papier-mâché to secure the fitting to the top of the boot. Finally, thread the red lace through the eyelets as you would a normal shoe. Take the ball of plasticine from the toe of the mould and press it into the toe of the now finished boot to weigh down the front.

If the colours we have used for our lamp base don't blend in with your child's bedroom, you may like to choose another range of colours that does. You may also wish to vary the decoration on the shoe — perhaps painting a picture of the Old Woman herself on one side, adding some flowers or more windows and so on.

JEWELLERY

DECORATED BEADS

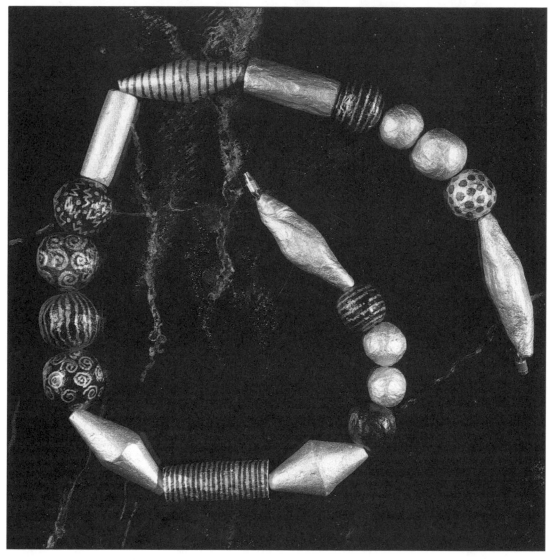

MATERIALS

To make the necklace shown *below left* you will need:

Above, 230g (8oz) packet of Pebeo wood pulp; knitting needles, 3.75mm (size 9) and 2.75mm (size 11); 50ml (2 fl oz) tin Ardenbrite gold paint; 125ml (5 fl oz) Ardenbrite protective glaze; black enamel paint; two paint brushes, one medium and one fine; bowl.

Above, flat, coarse hand file; two sheets of sandpaper, fine and medium grade; plasticine; white spirit (for cleaning brushes); fine nylon line and necklace catch (available from department stores); rubber gloves; kitchen knife; scissors.

In previous projects we have used papier-mâché to make decorative and utilitarian objects for the home. Here we show you how to use this material to make a sophisticated bead necklace for personal adornment.

For this papier-mâché project you can either use a commercially-produced papier-mâché (generally called wood pulp) or a home-made one. If you would like to try making your own, you should be able to find a reference book on the subject in your local library.

The disadvantages of using home-made papier-mâché for beads is that it takes a lot longer to dry, and if you accelerate the process by drying the material in the oven, even on the lowest heat, it is prone to shrinkage. It also has a rougher texture — which can sometimes be desirable — and if a smooth finish is required the process of sanding will take longer.

We have made our necklace of beads

with commercial wood pulp. This is easy to roll out and form into the desired shapes; home-made papier-mâché is difficult to roll and should instead be formed into separate small pieces.

When purchasing your enamel, gold paint and varnish (or protective glaze) do ensure that they are compatible; some varnishes will remove the gold paint when they are applied on top of it. For this reason we suggest you ask the stockist of gold paint whether it is affected by varnish. Even so, do a test yourself to ensure that the varnish does not 'melt' the gold paint. If you cannot find a varnish that does not dissolve the gold, you should leave the beads unvarnished.

HELPFUL HINT

To make a quick version of the necklace, make seven beads and thread them onto a silky piece of coloured cord about 50cm (20in) long, then knot the ends of the cord together.

1 Prepare the pulp according to the manufacturer's instructions. When the mixture is ready to use, take a small handful and roll it into an even sausage shape about 15mm (½in) in diameter. Measure off about 30mm (1in) and cut with a knife. Cut the rest of the roll into similar size pieces.

2 To make the cylindrical bead, smooth the cut ends with your fingers and gently roll the pulp out as before, until it is smooth and even again. Hold it firmly in one hand and carefully twist the 2.75mm (size 11) knitting needle through the centre until it emerges from the other end. Pull it back out and insert the larger needle in the opposite end. Push it all the way through and twist it round a few times before carefully pulling it back out.

HELPFUL HINT

By twisting the needle as it goes in and out of the bead you are less likely to distort the shape. While the larger needle is still in the bead, check that the shape is not distorted. If it is, re-shape while the bead is on the needle and then twist the needle out very carefully.

3 To make the round bead, roll out another sausage shape and cut it into lengths of approximately 30mm (1in). The shorter the length, the smaller the bead, so try different lengths. Take the cut piece in the palm of your hand and, with the other hand covering it, pulp it into a ball by using a circular motion. Carefully make the holes as described in Step 2.

4 To make the conical-shaped bead, repeat Step 3, but before you make the hole, knead the ball gently with the fingers of both hands, slowly drawing the bead into a taper at each end. Repeat the above steps until you have three cylindrical, twelve round and five conical beads. Place all the beads on a sheet of newspaper and leave them to dry thoroughly. This will take several days — the exact time will be determined by the wetness of the pulp, room temperature and humidity.

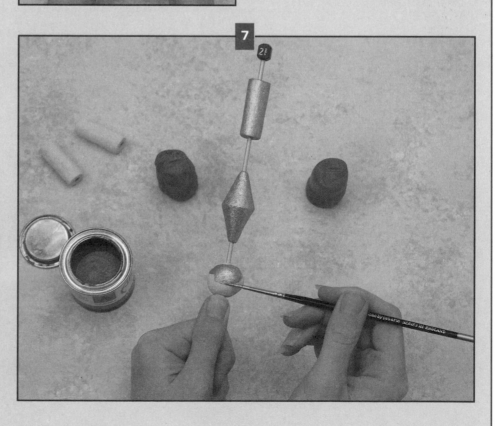

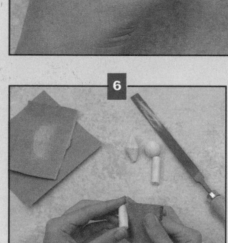

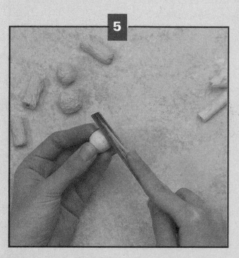

5 When the beads are dry, file them with a coarse file. Hold the bead in one hand and the file in the other, filing gently following the curve of the bead.

6 When you have evened out the surface with the coarse file, sand the bead gently to a smooth finish using first medium grade and then fine grade sandpaper. File and sand all the beads in the same way. The filing and sanding does not have to produce a perfect geometric bead, but you do need a smooth finish for the paint while retaining the hand-made character.

HELPFUL HINT

Filing and sanding the beads will produce a fine dust, so if you are sensitive to dust it is a good idea to wear a face mask while carrying out this part of the work.

7 To make painting the beads easier, take two pieces of plasticine and mould them into two 'towers' (rather like the pylons of a bridge). Use these to support the knitting needle while the paint is drying. Thread the beads that are to be painted gold on to a knitting needle and paint them with the gold paint. Leave to dry. Thread the remaining beads on another knitting needle and paint with the black paint. If necessary, apply a second coat.

8 When the base colour is completely dry, place a single bead on the large needle and, using a fine paint brush, paint on the design. Set it aside to dry. When you have painted all the beads and the paint has dried thoroughly, apply the varnish.

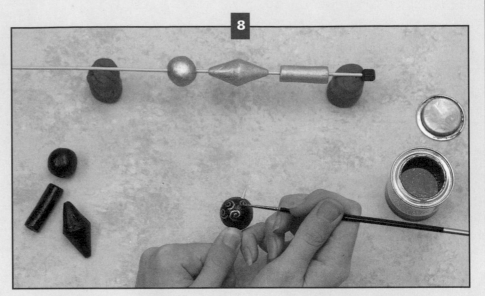

HELPFUL HINT

If you find it difficult to paint the gold patterns with a brush, you could use a gold marker pen. The same applies to the black patterns on the gold beads — a black permanent marker can be used instead of the brush and black paint. However, if you do use this method, you will not be able to varnish your beads.

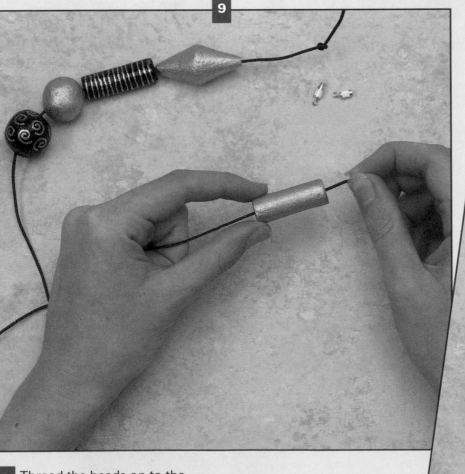

This project provides endless possibilities for variety and experimentation. You can make the beads in different shapes and any size you wish — they are very light, so even larger beads will not produce a heavy necklace — and paint them in the colours of your choice.

9 Thread the beads on to the required length of nylon thread. Knot each end and tie on to the catch.

PAPERCRAFT

ANTIQUE VASE

MATERIALS

To make the papier-mâché vase shown *below left* you will need:

Above, pear-shaped balloon; newspaper; wallpaper paste; container; tablespoon; masking tape; brush for paste; liquidiser; jam jar; sieve; small bowl; washing up bowl.

Above, felt-tip pen; scissors; cotton wool buds; white emulsion paint; lamp black water-soluble pigment; Humbrol enamel paint, blue and bronze; gloss polyurethane varnish; PVA (white) glue; white spirit.

Our antique vase with its decorative coiled motif is evocative of ancient ceramic and bronze treasure, yet is actually made of papier-mâché. The 'distressed' metallic finish is achieved with enamel paints.

We have already used the layering method — building up pasted strips of paper on a mould — in several earlier papier-mâché projects. In this project the basic form of the vase is built up by the same method, using a balloon as a mould, and then paper pulp is used for modelling the lip, foot and spiral decoration.

Making a papier-mâché form requires a certain amount of patience as each stage must be left to dry fully before proceeding to the next stage. By adding PVA (white) glue instead of wallpaper paste to the pulp, the drying time is speeded up slightly, and

the glue also gives increased adhesion.

When you reach the stage of adding paper pulp to the basic form you can speed up the drying time by placing the piece in an airing cupboard or near a radiator. However, do not be tempted to do this when the paper is drying on the balloon — the air inside may expand and burst the balloon. The structure is quite fragile in the early stages and so should be handled with some care.

Cover your work surface with plastic so that the piece does not stick to the table. This is particularly important when you are forming the lip on the vase.

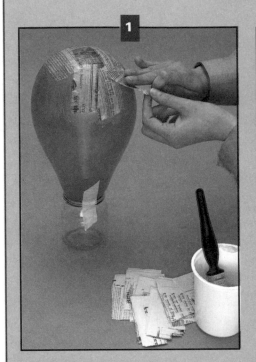

1 Blow up a balloon and tie the opening. Stick it with masking tape to a jam jar as shown, to hold it steady as you cover it. Add two tablespoons of wallpaper paste to a cup of water, mix well and leave to stand for 15 minutes. Tear several sheets of newspaper into pieces about 5cm (2in) square. Apply paste to both sides of the newspaper pieces with a brush or your fingers, and then stick pieces to the balloon, overlapping them and smoothing them down with your finger to remove air bubbles and excess paste.

2 Cover the balloon down to about 5cm (2in) from the bottom. Apply two further layers of paper and leave to dry overnight. Draw a line around the base of the paper, about 1cm (½in) from the edge, resting your hand on the washing up bowl to steady it, and rotating the balloon to get a straight line. Pop the balloon.

3 Make snips up to the line at 1cm (½in) intervals with a pair of scissors. Fold down the rim as shown.

4 To make the pulp, tear up about 20 sheets of newspaper and soak in a bowl of water overnight. Place a couple of handfuls of soaked paper in a liquidiser, add some water and process until the pieces are well broken up. Empty the mixture into a sieve and continue to process more batches of newspaper until the sieve is nearly full. Squeeze the mixture to remove the excess water, then place in a small bowl. Add one tablespoon of PVA (white) glue and mix well with a spoon.

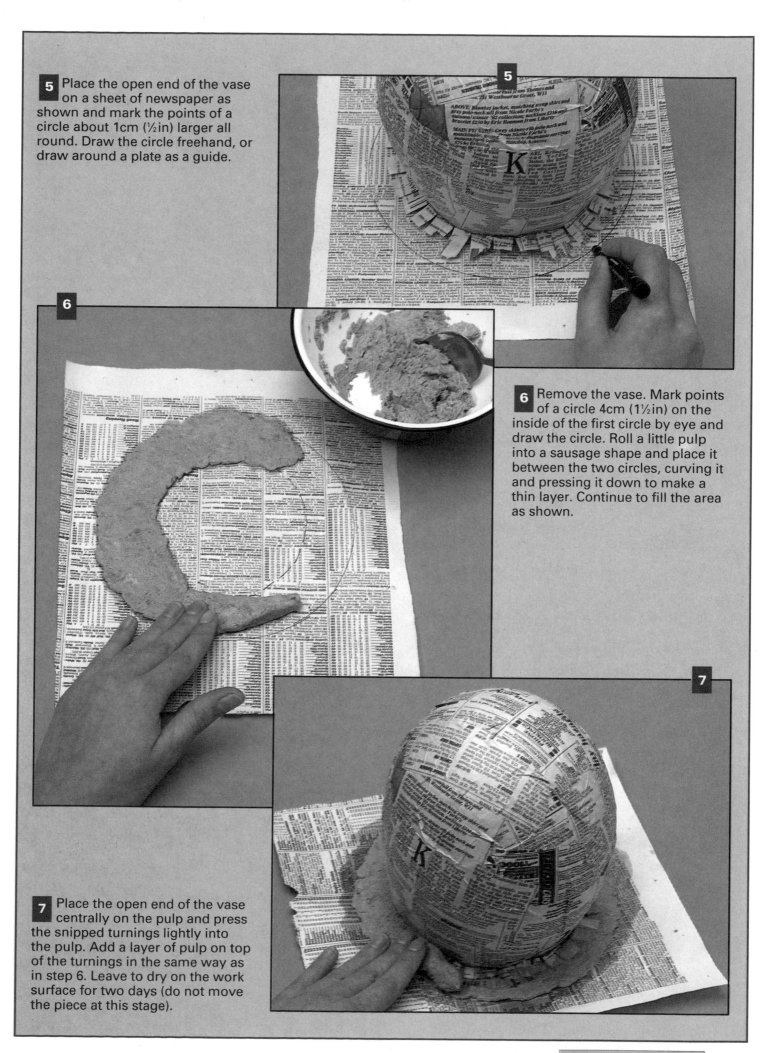

5 Place the open end of the vase on a sheet of newspaper as shown and mark the points of a circle about 1cm (½in) larger all round. Draw the circle freehand, or draw around a plate as a guide.

6 Remove the vase. Mark points of a circle 4cm (1½in) on the inside of the first circle by eye and draw the circle. Roll a little pulp into a sausage shape and place it between the two circles, curving it and pressing it down to make a thin layer. Continue to fill the area as shown.

7 Place the open end of the vase centrally on the pulp and press the snipped turnings lightly into the pulp. Add a layer of pulp on top of the turnings in the same way as in step 6. Leave to dry on the work surface for two days (do not move the piece at this stage).

8 Remove from the table and turn over. Cut into the centre of the paper (to make the vase easier to handle) and trim the outer paper to within 2cm (¾in) of the pulp rim. Add a thin layer of pulp on the top side of the rim to match the pulp rim beneath. Leave to dry. Turn over the outer edges of the newspaper and paste them to the underside of the rim, adding more pieces to cover the rim. Cut away the newspaper inside the top of the vase. Leave to dry overnight in a warm place.

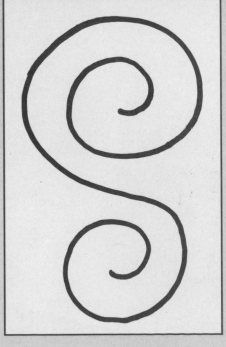

9 At the centre of the base of the vase, build a small circular foot using a thin sausage of pulp. Using the decoration guide as reference (see box), draw a series of freehand spirals around the bowl with a felt-tip pen as shown.

10 Build up the spiral designs with thin sausages of pulp. Press the pulp gently on to the surface to make sure that it is well adhered. Leave to dry overnight.

THE DECORATION

11 Pour three tablespoons of white emulsion into a jam jar and add two tablespoons of black pigment and a teaspoon of water. Mix together well with a brush.

12 Paint the inside of the vase and the top of the rim with this grey mix and leave to dry for an hour. Paint the outside and the base of the vase and leave to dry.

13 Use cotton wool buds to apply blue enamel paint around the edges of the raised spiral designs. Leave to dry for half an hour.

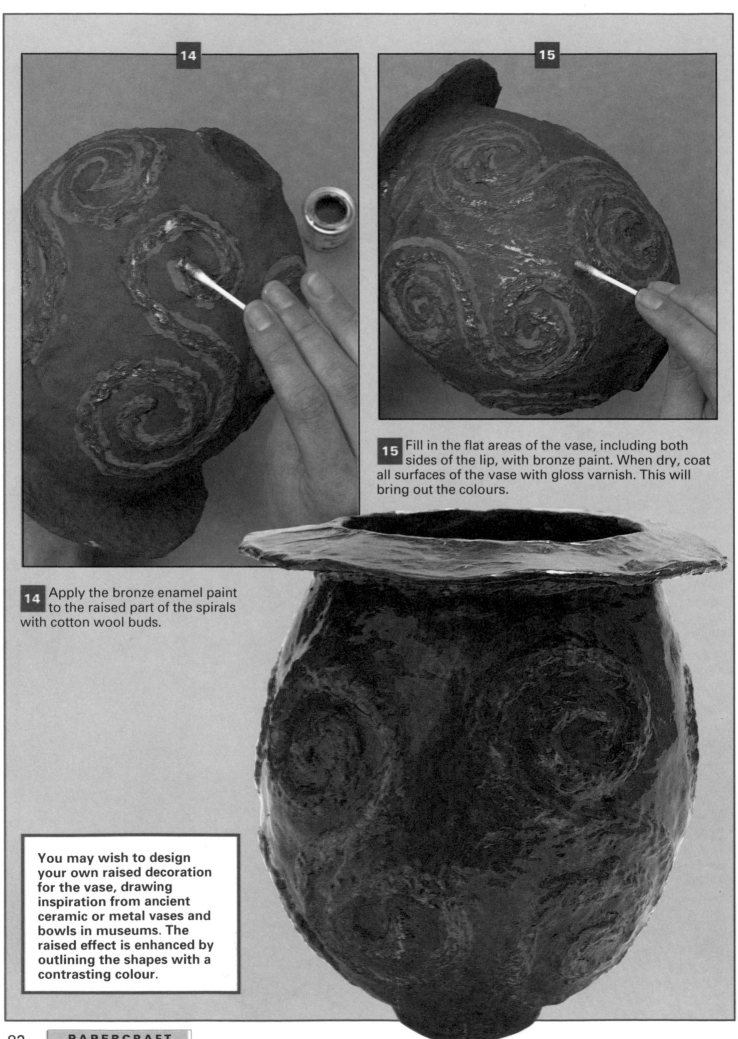

15 Fill in the flat areas of the vase, including both sides of the lip, with bronze paint. When dry, coat all surfaces of the vase with gloss varnish. This will bring out the colours.

14 Apply the bronze enamel paint to the raised part of the spirals with cotton wool buds.

You may wish to design your own raised decoration for the vase, drawing inspiration from ancient ceramic or metal vases and bowls in museums. The raised effect is enhanced by outlining the shapes with a contrasting colour.

MARBLED PAPER

Oil marbling is one of the most direct techniques employed to make decorated papers. The reaction of oil colour and water in its simplest form provides a fascinating medium for achieving original decorative results.

MATERIALS

To make the marbled papers shown *below left* you will need:

Above, small plastic bucket; plastic tray, approximately 30 x 37cm (12 x 15in); cellulose wallpaper paste; wooden spoon or mixing stick; sheets of white A4 (11¹¹⁄₁₆ x 8¼in) paper; newsprint or newspaper, to protect your work surface.

The history of marbled papers has long been associated with Asia, especially the Far East. The earliest examples of decorative marbling can be traced back to the Japanese, who were making use of them as early as the 8th century. Subtly marked marbled papers, known as suminagashi, were used for calligraphy. The paper was partially marbled in selected areas, perhaps as an early form of authenticating documents.

Extensive use of marbling was made in Persia and Turkey around the 16th century, notably as part of the integral design and decoration on miniature paintings and illuminated manuscripts. With the advent of merchants operating actively in the Middle East and Asia, sheets of marbled paper became increasingly available. At this time they were used mainly to line the interiors of boxes, bound eventually for the European market, and subsequently the art of marbling reached the western world. More recently, marbled papers have been associated with the art of bookbinding, and are the classic medium for decorated endpapers. Today marbling is applied to a broader field, taking in packaging and gift wrap as well as pure decorative art.

The traditional method of marbling paper relies on the process of floating watercolour (mixed with ox gall, which acts as a floating agent) on the surface of a thickened size made of Irish moss (carragheen moss). Here we have replaced watercolours with student quality oil paints. The size is made from a cellulose wallpaper paste to provide a more direct process for making handmade marbled papers.

Although you will find that the marbling takes very little time, you will have to allow about 24 hours for your prints to dry. Once they are thoroughly dry you can, if you wish, place them under several heavy books to press them flat.

Above, student's oil paints in blue, red, yellow, black and green; four glass jars; white spirit; three paint brushes, size 6; four glass droppers or pipettes.

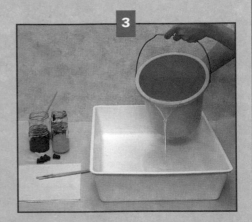

1 For the base liquid, or 'bath', mix up the wallpaper paste and water in a small plastic bucket, following the manufacturer's directions and adding more water if necessary until the mixture is the consistency of single cream. Stir all the time as you mix to make certain the paste is kept free of lumps.

2 Cover your work surface with newsprint or newspaper and mix the oil colour by squeezing out 2cm (1in) of paint into a clean glass jar. Using a dropper or pipette, add a few drops of white spirit and stir with a paint brush until the paint has dissolved. Continue to add white spirit until the mixture is thin enough to be drawn up into the dropper. Mix three or four other colours in the same way.

3 Transfer your base liquid to a plastic tray, filling the tray to a minimum depth of 5cm (2in). Arrange the jars of paint, paper for marbling and droppers close to the tray of paste.

4 Draw up some blue colour into the dropper and drop a few spots on to the surface of the bath. Rock the tray to and fro a few times to allow the paint to disperse a little. Add a few more drops of colour and swirl the paint with a paint brush.

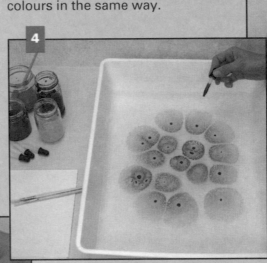

5 When the colour has spread evenly on the surface, add a few drops of red colour. Gently swirl again with a paint brush, then allow the paint to spread and settle for a few seconds.

HELPFUL HINT

If the paint sinks to the bottom of the tray after it has been dropped on to the surface of the base liquid it is too thick, and you will have to dilute it further with white spirit. If, however, you have diluted it too much the paint will disperse too quickly on the surface and you will have to add more paint to the diluted solution.

6 Gently lay your first piece of paper on the water by dropping one of the corners on to the surface of the bath and then releasing the paper to float on the surface.

7 Leave the paper in the bath for a few seconds, then remove it carefully by two corners. Lay the paper out on a piece of newspaper and leave to dry for about 24 hours.

8 To achieve a mottled effect, rather than the more traditional marbled one, let a few drops of black disperse on the surface of the bath and leave for one minute. If you wish, you can rock the tray a little to help the colour disperse.

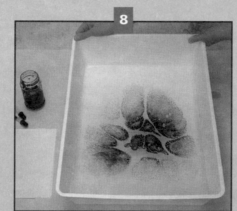

HELPFUL HINT

When you place your paper on the bath, make certain there are no air bubbles trapped underneath the paper; if there are, gently tap the bubbles from the back of the paper to release the air. If the air bubbles are left they will create white areas on the marbling.

CHANGING COLOURS

If you want to print with different colours, you will need to clear the surface of the bath of existing colour. To do this, lay a piece of newsprint or newspaper — cut to the size of the bath — on top of the bath, and repeat two to three times with fresh paper until all the excess paint has been removed. The bath can be cleaned in this way time after time.

9 Using a small brush, delicately spot a second colour on to the surface, then add a third colour. A number of colours can be used in this way; some will merge to give extra colours to enrich the marbling.

10 When you are satisfied with the result, take another print.

11 More subtle marbling can be achieved by leaving the residue of previous colours in the tray and adding a few drops of white spirit to the surface of the liquid. Agitate the bath with the paint brush to give a softer result, and then take your print.

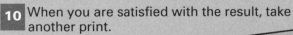

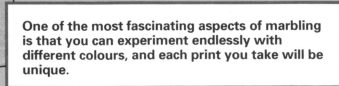

One of the most fascinating aspects of marbling is that you can experiment endlessly with different colours, and each print you take will be unique.

PRINTMAKING

ROLLER PRINTING

MATERIALS

To make the roller printed paper shown *below left* you will need:

Above, wooden rolling pin; A4 (11¾ x 8¼in) sheet of paper; A4 (11¾ x 8¼in) sheet of carbon paper; large and medium sized U-shaped lino cutting tools; A3 (16½ x 11¾in) cutting mat; craft knife; masking tape; 3H pencil; fine black felt-tip pen; metal ruler.

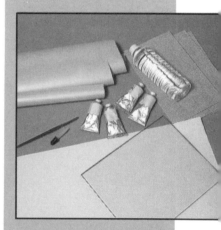

Above, A2 (23⅜ x 16½in) sheet of lightweight cartridge paper; 12 sheets of A1 (33⅛ x 23⅜in) newsprint; sheet of glass for inking; oil-based printing inks: orange, vermilion, cobalt blue and white; small paintbrush; small pipette; white spirit; 3 all-purpose or cotton cloths.

In this project we introduce you to a novel printmaking technique that is based on ancient cylinder seals. A design is carved on to an ordinary wooden rolling pin which, when dabbed with random colours, can be used to decorate large areas of paper quickly and distinctively.

Our roller-printing project is inspired by the cylinder seals which were used by the ancient Syrians to imprint designs on to wet clay. The Syrians used materials such as ivory and alabaster to make their seals, but we have adapted the method to an inexpensive object — a wooden rolling pin.

Hand crafted

Items hand-printed from wood have a unique appeal. In this project the random inking and the pressure exerted on the roller make each print slightly different. For our design we have taken a theme from Indian ceramic tile designs, which are based on stylised flower, plant and wildlife forms. When printed with a roller the design forms a continuous composition of repeated shapes — indeed, this method was traditionally used for producing patterned wallpaper before the introduction of machinery for mass-production.

We have provided a template pattern for the project, but you can of course make up your own designs. The most important thing is to measure the circumference of the roller accurately so that when drawing up your design you can ensure that the top and bottom edges will join up to form a continuous pattern.

When printing a large sheet of paper you may find that the colour strength appears uneven. A more even print can be achieved by rolling each section in alternate directions — from top to bottom, then bottom to top. It is also a good idea to place your paper on a thick wad of newsprint; this acts as a cushion for the roller and helps to produce a strong impression.

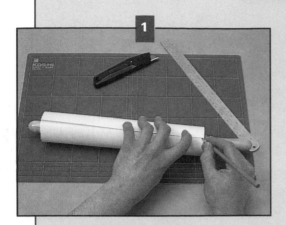

1 Wrap the sheet of A4 (11¾ x 8¼ in) paper tightly around the rolling pin and mark off with a pencil the exact length and circumference of the roller. Lay the paper on a cutting mat and cut it to size with a craft knife and metal ruler. Cut a sheet of carbon paper to the same size.

2 Photocopy the template and enlarge it to fit the sheet of paper, making sure the two long edges form a continuous design when matched up. Wrap the carbon paper, carbon side down, tightly around the rolling pin and secure it with small pieces of masking tape. Wrap the design around in the same way, securing it to the rolling pin with small pieces of masking tape.

3 With a 3H pencil, trace around the edges of the black lines to transfer the design onto the rolling pin. Concentrate on one small section at a time, and hold the rolling pin firmly to prevent it slipping.

TEMPLATE

The length of **x** should equal the circumference of your rolling pin.

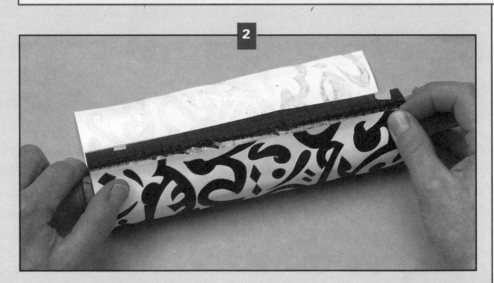

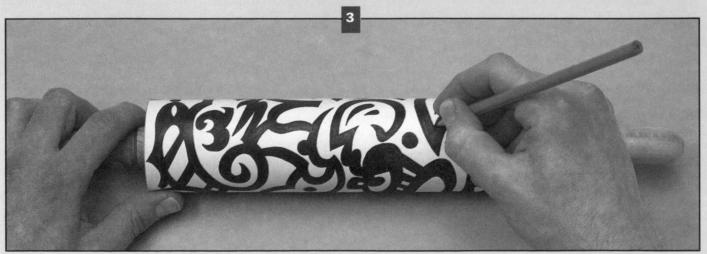

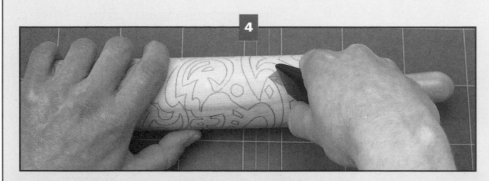

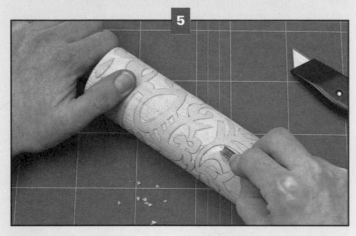

4 Remove the design and carbon paper and check that the tracing has come out clearly. Strengthen any weak lines with a black felt-tip pen. Using the tip of a sharp craft knife, carefully score all the lines. Keep the rolling pin as steady as possible while cutting and work on small areas at a time.

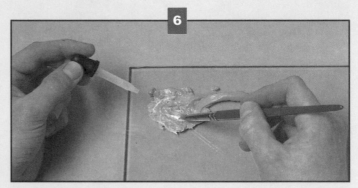

5 Using the large U-shaped lino cutting tool, gouge out the 'negative' areas between the black lines of the design to a depth of a millimetre or so. Use the medium sized U-shaped tool for the smaller areas. Always cut towards the scored lines.

6 Place 12 sheets of A1 (33⅛ x 23⅜in) newsprint on the work surface and secure a sheet of A2 (23⅜ x 16½in) cartridge paper to it with masking tape at each corner. Squeeze 10cm (4in) of orange and 2cm (1in) of white oil-based printing inks on to the glass sheet and mix together with a small paintbrush. Use the pipette to dispense enough white spirit on to the ink to thin it to the consistency of single cream.

7 On separate areas of the glass sheet, mix vermilion and white, and then cobalt blue and white, in the same way. Crumple a cloth into a ball and use it to dab orange ink randomly all over the cut surface of the rolling pin. The ink should be thick but not runny.

8 Repeat the random dabbing of colour with the red and the blue inks, using a separate cloth for each colour. Ensure that the raised parts of the design are completely covered with colour.

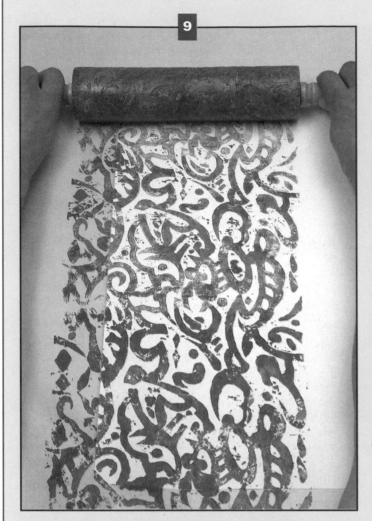

9

9 The paper is printed in three sections. Start by placing the rolling pin at the bottom left of the cartridge paper, overlapping the edges by 5cm (2in). Slowly roll up to the top edge, keeping the rolling pin as straight as possible.

10 Re-ink the rolling pin in the same way as before (you do not need to clean it first). Position the rolling pin at the top of the paper, as close as possible to the edge of the first printing, and roll down to the bottom edge.

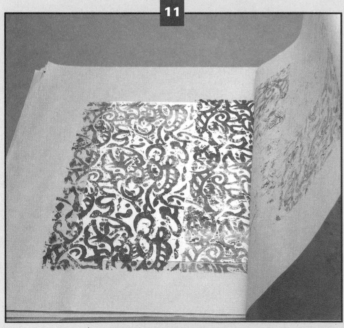

11 Re-ink the rolling pin and print the last section of the paper, working from bottom to top. Blot the print with a sheet of newsprint to remove any excess ink and leave it to dry for at least 24 hours. When you have finished printing clean the rolling pin and the glass sheet with a cloth and white spirit.

You can use your roller printer to make your own original gift wrap and matching tags, or to decorate book jackets. Have fun experimenting with inks in different colour combinations and on a variety of coloured papers.

SURFACE DECORATION

DECOUPAGE

A plain wooden box can be transformed into an exotic, richly decorated object by using the Victorian art of decoupage. The sophistication of the final effect belies the simplicity of the techniques involved.

Decoupage, from the French word 'couper' (to cut), is the decoration of objects using cut-out printed paper images which are pasted on to the artefact and heavily coated with varnish.

The technique was originally developed in the 18th century as a cheap and accessible way of imitating oriental lacquerwork, which was then all the rage in Europe. In the 19th century it became a popular pastime for ladies, and many fine examples dating from this period still exist today.

The sources for cut-out designs are virtually limitless: magazines, photographs, newspapers, flower catalogues, posters, postcards, birthday cards. You can also buy sheets of specially-designed decoupage images. We have chosen to combine cut-outs from reproductions of fabric and wallpaper designs by William Morris with a paisley pattern border. These were taken from books but you could use real wallpaper samples and wrapping paper as a cheaper alternative. When selecting your images, remember that it is the intricate cut-out motifs such as birds, flowers, figures and animals that will give your work the traditional characteristic appearance of the technique. Thin paper is easier to apply than thick paper, but it does tend to stretch more when wet.

The varnish is stained with a little burnt umber oil paint to give an antique effect. There are no rules about the number of layers of varnish to apply. If you want to disguise the edges of the paper cut-outs then you may need up to twenty coats of varnish (depending on the thickness of the paper). A total of eight coats gives a very durable finish, and the edges of the cut-outs will create an interesting surface.

MATERIALS

To make the decoupage box shown *below left* you will need:

Above, wooden box (see Helpful hint *below*); fine sandpaper; selection of decorative coloured papers; scissors, large and small; ruler; pencil.

Above, PVA (white) glue; cloth; acrylic paint, Venetian red; oil paint, burnt umber; paintbrushes, round size 14, ¹/₄in flat, ³/₄in flat; saucer; turpentine; polyurethane gloss varnish.

HELPFUL HINT

You may already have an old box that is of a suitable size. Before you begin the decoupage, sand the box down to remove all finishes, and fill any holes. The box can then be sealed and painted, or stained and sealed again, before the cut-outs are glued on. You could also use a metal box - the treatment is exactly the same, but any rust must first be removed with wire wool and a rust inhibitor applied before the cut-outs are stuck on.

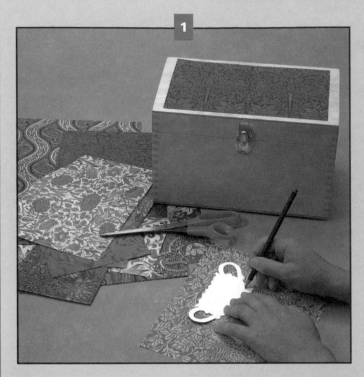

TEMPLATE

1 From your range of papers, select patterns for the backgrounds. We have chosen different patterns for the top, front and back of the box, and the same pattern for both sides. Cut the pieces of paper so that they are approximately 1cm (½ in) smaller all round than each surface of the box to be covered. Photocopy the template for the urn at 154%, then use the small scissors to cut around the shape. Trace around the shape on to a piece of decorative paper (you will need 3 urn shapes: for the top, front and back). Carefully cut out the urn shapes using the small scissors.

2 Start planning the design, working on one side of the box at a time. Start with the top of the box, placing the urn in position and then carefully cutting out elements from the papers that appeal to you. We have chosen flowers and birds placed in a symmetrical arrangement.

3 If the box is varnished, 'key' the surface by lightly smoothing it with fine sandpaper so that the glue will stick well.

4 Dilute some PVA (white) glue in a jam jar (three parts water to one part glue). Apply glue to the top of the box and the back of the piece of background paper using the small flat brush. Stick the paper down; brush glue over the top and smooth it out well with your fingers to remove the air bubbles. Wipe off the excess glue with a damp cloth. Any tiny air bubbles that remain will dry flat.

5 Stick the decorative cut-outs on to the top of the box, again using plenty of glue on all the surfaces and wiping it off with the cloth.

6 Cut 4 strips of paper for the border. Here the border is approximately 2cm (¾in) wide on the top of the box, with a 5mm (¼in) turnover down the side of the lid. Cut a scalloped edge on one side of each strip, then stick the borders in position with the scalloped edges on the top of the box.

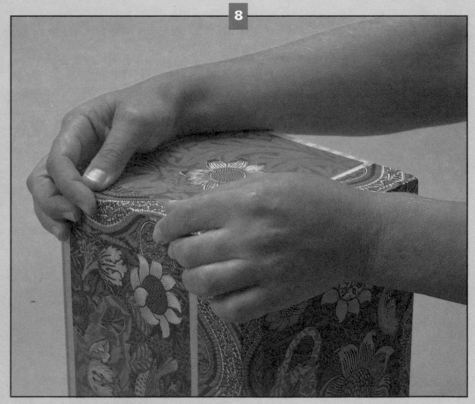

7 Cut 4 strips of paper to cover the sides of the lid, taking your measurements from the box. To make a neat finish around the metal clasp, cut a piece out of the paper strip the same shape as the clasp but a little smaller. Make small snips all round this shape and then place the strip in position. With a pencil draw around the clasp, then remove the strip and cut along this line with the small scissors. Cut around the hinges in the same way. Glue all the strips in position.

8 Continue working on the box, glueing all the pieces to one surface of the box before moving on to the next, and cutting around the clasps and hinges as described in step 7. Cut out strips of paper for the remaining borders, matching the pattern with the lid if necessary. These borders are about 2cm (1in) wide on all edges except the top, which is 1cm (⅜in) wide to balance with the border of the lid. Allow for a turnover of 5mm (¼in) on the border at the bottom of the box.

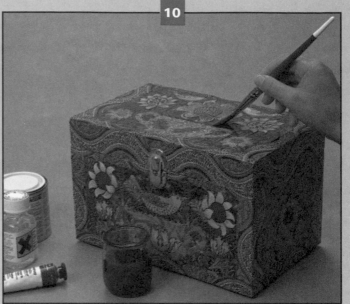

10 Squeeze a small amount — about 1cm (½in) — of burnt umber oil paint into a jam jar and dilute it with a little turpentine. Add varnish and mix well with a large, flat brush. Test the colour on a piece of white card — it should resemble the colour of black tea. Apply six coats of varnish to the box, leaving each coat to dry thoroughly before the next application. Between the two final coats, lightly rub the dry surface with fine sandpaper to achieve a glossy, lacquered effect.

9 Using the round paintbrush, paint the inside of the box with fairly thick acrylic paint, then paint carefully along the rims. Leave to dry, then apply a second coat to ensure even covering. Leave to dry. Paint the base of the box with two coats of acrylic paint.

You can apply decoupage decoration to any wood, metal or glass surface — a tray, mirror frame, or even a piece of furniture such as a table top, chest of drawers or screen.

PAPERCRAFT

QUILLING

MATERIALS

To make the decorated memo pad *below left* you will need:

Above, 4mm (⅛in) light blue mounting board at least 21 x 30cm (8½ x 12in); dark blue cartridge paper at least 21 x 21cm (8½ x 8½in); white A3 (16½ x 11¾in) cartridge paper, about 100gsm (45lb); quick-setting glue, eg Copydex; gummed fabric picture hanger for paper or board; notepad 10 x 15cm (4 x 6in).

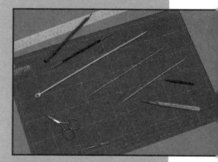

Above, scalpel; small paper scissors; quilling tool; 3 knitting needles, large, medium and small; pencil; steel ruler; tweezers; small paintbrush; needle; cutting board.

The lacy coils and scrolls that decorate our memo pad are an example of the ancient craft of quilling that is currently enjoying a revival of interest. We introduce you to the basic quilling technique and show you in detail how to complete your first quilling project successfully.

The craft of quilling involves rolling thin strips of paper into decorative coiled motifs and sticking these on a background so that the paper coils and scrolls are seen edge on.

Quilling is sometimes called paper filigree. It may have originated in ancient Egypt, but the first record of its use was in 15th-century Britain, when it was used by poor monastic orders as an effective imitation of gold and silver filigree work.

Drawing room craft
In the 18th and 19th centuries quilling became a popular pastime for ladies of leisure, who employed professional quilling masters to teach them the craft. Their quilling would be used to decorate small work boxes, screens, tea caddies and trays — the design would often be set within a frame and covered with glass to protect it.

Although it may appear an intricate and sophisticated craft, quilling is really quite simple. All you need are deft fingers and plenty of patience.

Scrolling technique
The basic rolling technique is easily mastered. One end of a long narrow strip of paper is inserted into the split end of the quilling tool, which is then rolled between the fingers. The resulting paper coil is removed from the tool and can then be used loose as it is, or formed into a scroll, or squashed or creased into a particular shape that is held in place with glue. The various coils, scrolls and shapes are then arranged into a final design and stuck down on a background, using quick-setting paper glue applied to the edge of the paper.

HELPFUL HINT

It can be rewarding to design your own quilling patterns – inspiration can be found from ornate metal work on gates as well as from more traditional sources found in museums.

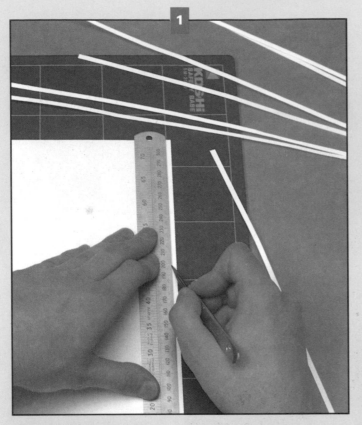

TEMPLATE FOR URN

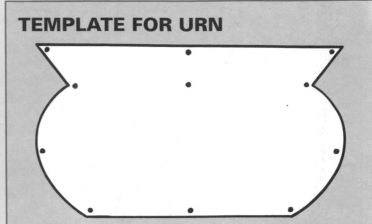

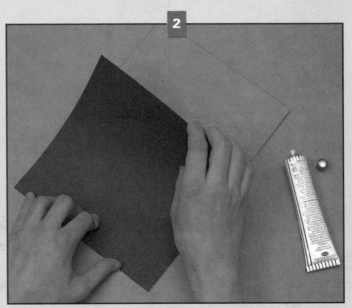

1 On one edge of the sheet of white cartridge paper mark intervals of 4mm (⅛in) with the pencil. Using the scalpel and steel ruler, cut the paper into strips.

2 Cut the light blue mounting board to 21 x 30cm (8½ x 12in). Cut a square of dark blue cartridge paper 21 x 21cm (8½ x 8½in). Spread glue on one side of the dark blue paper and stick to the mounting board, lining up the bottom and side edges carefully.

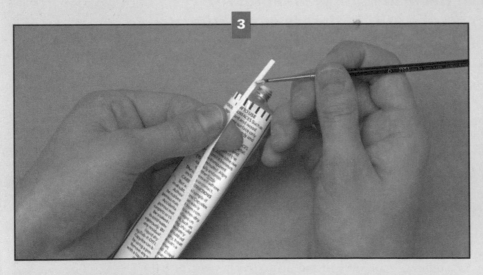

3 Cut four of the white cartridge paper strips to 208mm (8³⁄₁₆in). Take one strip and apply glue to one long edge with the paintbrush.

4 Glue the strip on its edge to the board, along the top of the cartridge square. Stretch the strip so that it is straight, and hold in place for about 20 seconds until it will stand on its own as the glue dries (you can hold one end with tweezers) Smooth in place with your fingers, and trim the ends with the scissors if necessary. Glue a second strip above the first, about 8mm (¼in) away, as shown. Glue two more strips at the top of the mounting board in the same way. For the side borders, first glue a strip 9cm (3½in) long along each side edge. Then cut two strips 74mm (3in) long for the inner borders and glue in place.

USING THE QUILLING TOOL

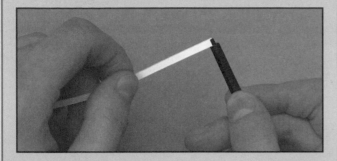

1 Fit one end of a paper strip in the notch in the quilling tool.

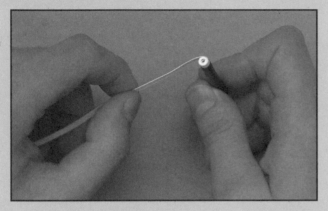

2 Revolve the quilling tool with your fingers to coil the paper strip.

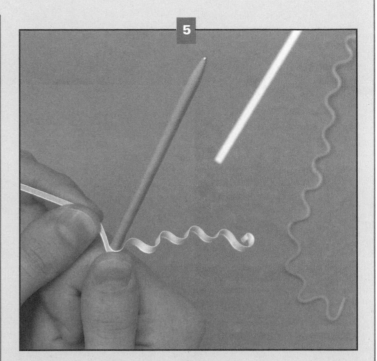

5 To make the borders, take a cartridge strip about 32cm (13in) long and fit one end into the quilling tool (see box). Make one or two turns to make a tight curl at the end, then remove from the quilling tool. Bend the strip backwards and forwards over a large knitting needle to make a wavy line, as shown.

6 Trim the length of the wavy strip to fit in one of the long borders. Curl the straight end with the quilling tool. Apply glue to the edge of the strip as before and glue in place, holding the strip in place with the tweezers and your fingers for about 20 seconds until the glue dries. Make the remaining wavy borders in the same way and glue in place.

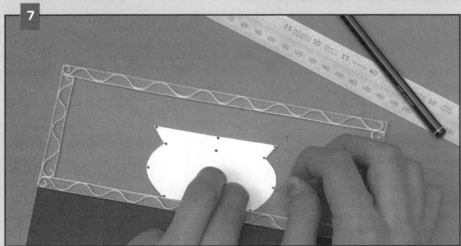

7 Photocopy the template for the urn same size and cut it out. Mark the centre of the bottom border and lay the template in place, matching up the centre marks. With the needle, make pinpricks in the card around the edge of the template where marked, and through the centre hole on the neck of the urn. Remove the template.

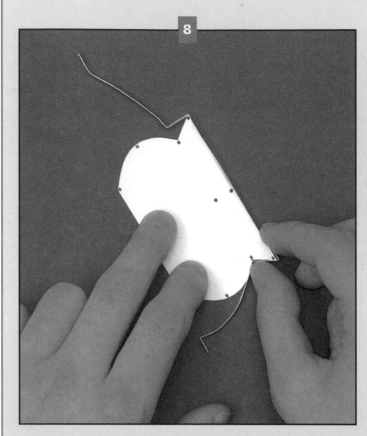

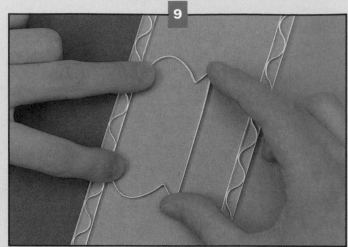

8 Cut a cartridge strip 20.5cm (8in) long. Bend it to fit around the shape of the urn, using the template as a guide. Bend back two tabs at the base to glue to the border.

9 Apply glue to the edge of the urn strip with the paintbrush as before, and then glue the urn outline in position, using the pinpricks as a guide, and glueing the bottom tabs to the border strip. Hold in position until dry.

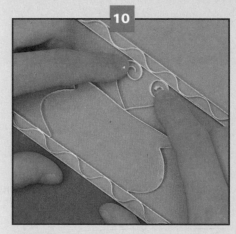

10 To make the heart shape above the urn, take a strip 14cm (5½in) long and bend in half. Curl the ends inwards using the quilling tool or a small knitting needle. Glue the edge of the strip and stick in place.

11 For the handles of the urn, use strips 11cm (4½in) long. Bend to shape using the quilling tool, rolling the ends in opposite directions as shown. Glue in place. Then cut a straight strip 6.5cm (2½in) long to fit under the rim of the urn. Glue in place.

12 For the little scrolls along the top of the urn cut five strips each 6cm (2½in) long. Coil each one tightly with the quilling tool and put a dab of glue at the end of the strip to hold the coil in place. Apply glue with the paintbrush to the back of each coil and, using tweezers, glue carefully in place along the top of the urn.

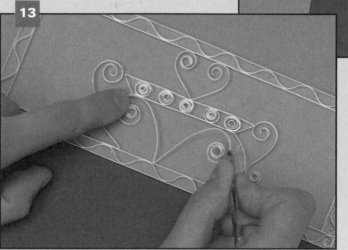

13 To make the central V motif on the urn, cut a strip 22cm (9in) long. Fold in half. Scroll each end round a medium sized knitting needle to make coils in opposite directions. Check that it fits into the urn shape, and glue in place.

HELPFUL HINT

To give a gentle curve to the stems, hold the cartridge strip behind an upright knitting needle with the first finger of your left hand and pull the strip through with your right hand.

15 To make the oval coils on the urn either side of the V, cut two strips 15cm (6in) long. First give a gentle curve to the whole strip (see Helpful Hint). Then put a spot of glue on one end and coil to make a tiny circle. Continue coiling, making a larger oval each time and putting a spot of glue at the base of each coil to hold the shape together. Glue in place.

14 To complete the decoration inside the urn, cut strips to the following lengths. For the scroll at the base of the V: 9cm (3½in); for the scroll at the top of the V: 15cm (6in); for the two bottom scrolls: 8cm (3in); for the two outer scrolls: 6cm (2½in). For the stems around the urn cut two strips 10.5cm (4in) for the lower stems and two strips 8.5cm (3½in) for the upper stems. Make up the scrolls and stems as shown and glue down.

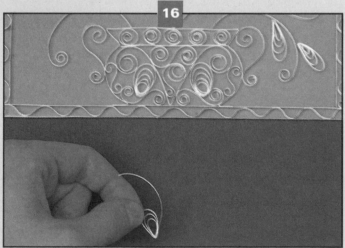

16 To make the leaves, cut eight strips 15cm (6in) long. The two top outer leaves (see step 17) have three curls, and all the rest have four curls. Make the leaves as described in step 15, but pinch the bottom of each leaf between your fingers to make it leaf shaped. Glue on the leaves in the positions shown in step 17.

17 Cut eight strips 6cm (2½in) long and 2cm (¾in) wide. Hold two strips together and make closely spaced scissor cuts across almost the whole width as shown. Separate the strips. Glue the uncut band and roll up to make a flower.

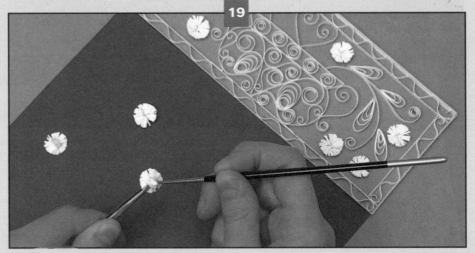

18 Open up the petals and trim to 1.5cm (½in) diameter.

19 Put a dab of glue in the centre back of each flower and glue in place.

20 Spread glue over the back of the notepad and glue in place. Attach the fabric picture hanger to the back of the card.

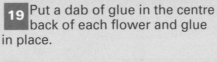

Once you have mastered the quilling technique you can make up your own designs. Try using different coloured papers and backgrounds — or for a rich effect you could spray the finished design with gold or silver paint to imitate precious filigree work.

PAPERCRAFT

PAPERCUT PICTURE

MATERIALS

To make the papercut shown *below left* you will need:

Above, sheet of 300gsm (140lb) watercolour paper; sheets of poster paper: black, purple, white.

Above, embroidery scissors; scalpel; glue stick; long steel ruler; cutting mat; 4H pencil; grey wax-free graphite tracing down paper; paper clips.

Our papercut picture is inspired by the work of 19th-century Swiss papercut artists and is intended to extend your papercraft skills. The symmetrical design is based on rural motifs and is dominated by a central image of a heart.

As with many crafts that use inexpensive materials, papercutting is common to many folk cultures. It is seen in the vibrant, colourful, many-layered papercut designs from Poland, that often depict flowers and birds, and in the intricate Mexican cut tissue squares that are hung from ceilings as festival decorations.

The early American settlers carried on the craft of their European forebears with papercuts embellished with text and painting, and these were often made to commemorate a birth or wedding, or some other important family occasion.

Rural life

Our design was inspired by the work of 19th century Swiss papercut artists working in the mountainous regions, who often depicted scenes of everyday rural life. The papercut is made in the traditional style, like a silhouette from black paper, and mounted on a white background. The design looks intricate and sophisticated,

but is in fact very simple as the main image is cut from a folded piece of paper of one colour. The border is made in reversed tones, white on black. A touch of colour is given by the purple squares at the corners.

Papercutting is a wonderful way of exploiting the symmetry of a design, and the heart image is a good example. The template is of half the final image. Make sure that you line up the edge with the fold of the paper, and trace and cut accurately. The main skill required is dexterity — small sharp embroidery scissors are used, and the cuts should be precise.

The poster paper used for the designs is very thin and easy to fold and cut. The paper is not dyed but has the colour printed on to one side. The back of the paper is always white which makes it easy to see the transferred design for cutting. Poster paper should be handled with care as it can be easily marked; you can buy a protective cardboard tube to store it in. Poster paper can be purchased from good art shops.

THE TEMPLATES (all measurements in mm: 25mm = 1in)

170

190

280

central motif

short border

flower design

long border

1 Cut a piece of watercolour paper 30 x 39cm (12 x 15½in). From the black poster paper cut a piece 25.5 x 19cm (10 x 7½in), two strips 5 x 30cm (2 x 12in) and two strips 5 x 39cm (2 x 15½in). From the purple poster paper cut four squares 4.5 x 4.5cm (1¾ x 1¾in). From the white poster paper cut two strips 19 x 5cm (7½ x 2in) and 28 x 5cm (11 x 2in). Fold the four white strips in half lengthways, right side in. Enlarge the template for the central motif on a photocopier at 200%, the borders at 200%, and the flower at 100%.

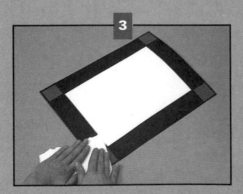

2 Apply glue to the back of the long pieces of black paper and stick on the watercolour background. Stick the two shorter pieces of black paper in position.

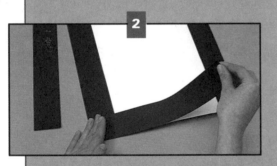

3 Stick the purple squares in place. Using a scrap of paper to protect the paper of the design, rub down over the whole surface with your hand to create a flat base.

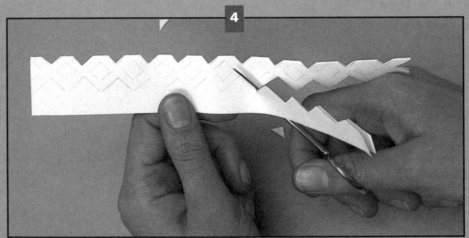

4 Cut a piece of grey graphite paper to 2.5 x 19cm (1 x 7½in). Place it on one of the shorter white folded papers, place the template for the short border design on top, lining up the edge with the fold, and secure with two paper clips. With a pencil, go over the outline of the design to transfer it to the paper. Remove the paper clips. Cut out the triangular shapes and the zig-zag outline with scissors.

5 Cut the inside shapes with a scalpel. Transfer and cut the second short border in the same way. Transfer and cut out the design for the long border on the two folded long pieces of white paper.

6 Flatten the borders with your fingers to remove the creases, glue the back of the paper and stick in position on the black borders as shown.

HELPFUL HINT

When cutting intricate shapes out of folded paper, always hold the paper close to the area to be cut so that both folds are cut accurately. Use the point of the knife to lift out the small pieces that are cut away. When cutting curves, hold the scissors and turn the paper, rather than turning the scissors.

7 Fold the remaining piece of black poster paper in half as shown, with the black surface innermost. Cut a piece of graphite paper to 19 x 13cm (7½ x 5in). Place the poster paper on the table with the fold on the right, place the graphite paper and the enlarged central motif template on the paper (lining up the edge accurately with the fold) and secure together with paper clips. Go over the lines of the template with a pencil.

8 Remove the template and graphite paper and cut carefully around the outlines of the design as shown, leaving the area between the tree and the rabbit until last. Hold the folded paper together firmly as you cut.

9 When you have cut all around the outline, use a scalpel to cut out the inside shapes, starting with the spaces between the legs of the rabbit and bird.

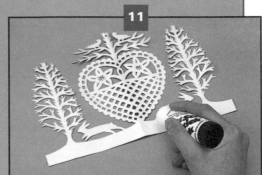

10 Cut away the shapes along the fold of the paper with the scalpel, and then cut out the shapes inside the heart.

11 Unfold the finished design and gently press out the crease. Dab glue on the back of the design, taking care not to damage the paper.

12 Lift the design carefully and place it on the watercolour paper, lining up the base of the central motif with one of the long black borders. With your fingers, gently smooth down the base, then the centre of the heart, the trunks of the trees (working from the bottom to the top), the rest of the heart, the rabbits, and finally the branches.

13 Cut four pieces of white poster paper, 6 x 6cm (2½ x 2½in). Stack them on top of one another, place the flower design on the top and secure with a paper clip. Cut through all thicknesses around the outline. Using the template as a guide, cut the pieces from the inside as shown. Stick one flower in each purple corner.

You can mount and frame your finished papercut to make an attractive picture to hang on the wall. You could also use the heart motif alone on a coloured background to make a distinctive Valentine's Day card.

JEWELLERY

PAPER AND SILVER EARRINGS

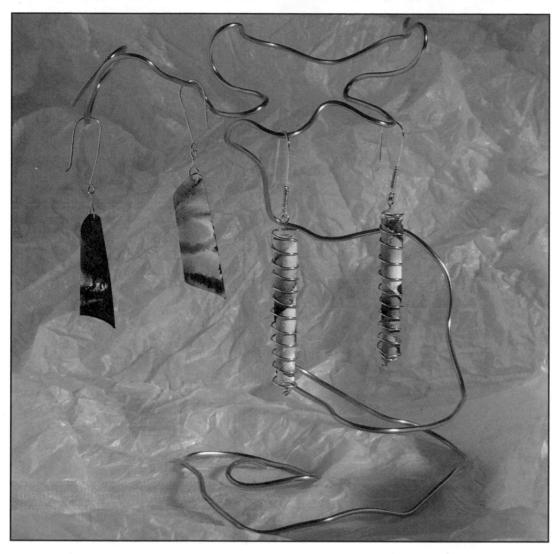

MATERIALS

To make the rolled paper earrings shown *below left* you will need:

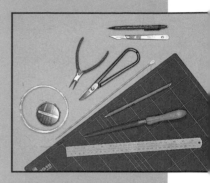

Above, ½m (½yd) of 0.7mm (¹⁄₃₂in) gauge round silver wire; approximately 15cm (6in) of 0.4mm (¹⁄₆₄in) gauge round silver wire; round-nosed pliers; tin snips; 15cm (6in) half round medium grade ring file; scalpel; cutting mat; metal ruler; knitting needle; round-barrelled pencil; 2 sewing needles, fine and thick; ballpoint pen.

Above, sheet of 185gsm (90lb) watercolour paper; watercolour paints: cadmium yellow, Prussian blue and scarlet lake; small round watercolour brush; palette; dinner plate; jam jar; glue; matt varnish; turpentine.

Our unusual and colourful earrings — reminiscent of tiny Chinese lanterns — are made from pieces of hand-painted paper rolled into narrow tubes and wrapped round with coils of delicate silver wire.

Jewellery-making doesn't necessarily require a high degree of skill or expensive equipment — as this project demonstrates. Paper earrings are easy and fun to make — and surprisingly strong and hard-wearing. They also have the advantage that, being so light, they have plenty of movement but do not pull on the ear lobes as metal earrings can do.

Our earrings are made from triangular pieces of watercolour paper decorated with watercolour paints, then rolled into tubes and coated with matt varnish to make them rain-proof. If you wish, the earrings can be left like this, with the ear wires slotted through holes at one end of the tube; but the addition of coiled silver wire gives them an added touch of sophistication.

Because paper earrings are so simple and inexpensive to make, there is plenty of scope for variation. For example, you can vary the dimensions and angles of the paper triangles to produce either long, pendulous earrings or small, compact ones. And, of course, you can experiment with different patterns and colours to decorate the paper coils; choose between vivid colours and bold patterns, or the understated elegance of neutral hues.

Instead of rolling the paper into a narrow tube you could curl it around a length of thick dowelling to make a more open shape, as illustrated at the end of the project. Remember that if you do this you will need to paint both sides of the paper, as the inner surface of the earrings will be visible.

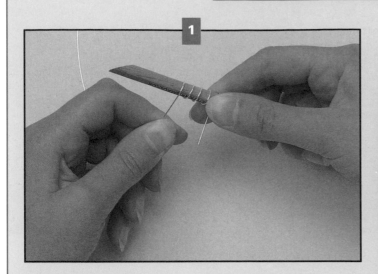

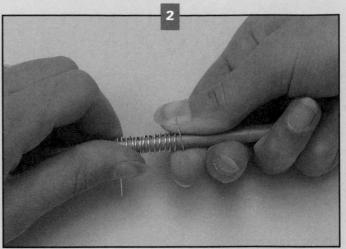

1 To make the silver coils, take the 0.7mm (1/32in) gauge silver wire and, leaving a 2cm (3/4in) end free, begin wrapping it around the pencil. Holding the wire taut all the time, form 12 evenly spaced loops, about 4mm (1/8in) apart.

2 Snip off the rest of the wire, again leaving a 2cm (3/4in) end free. Bunch up the loops and, with the two ends held between thumb and forefinger, twist in opposite directions to tighten up the coil and prevent it from working loose.

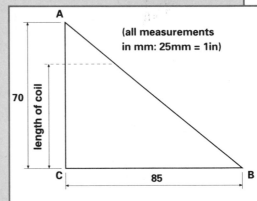

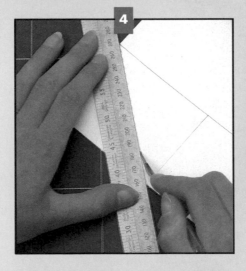

(all measurements in mm: 25mm = 1in)

A

length of coil 70

C — 85 — B

3 Slip the wire coil off the pencil. At one end, twist the free 2cm (3/4in) of wire to make first one small circle, then another slightly larger one. Do this by curling the end of the wire around one prong of the pliers, then continue curling around both prongs. Repeat steps 1-3 to make the coil for the other earring.

4 In a corner of the watercolour paper, cut out a rectangle 85 x 70mm (3 3/8in x 2 3/4in), then cut it in half diagonally to form two triangles (see diagram *above right*).

5 Soak the paper triangles in water for a minute or so to remove the surface coating. Meanwhile, dilute some Prussian blue and cadmium yellow paint to a watery consistency on the palette. Lay a triangle on the dinner plate and apply alternate blotches of blue and yellow paint to the edge AB. Drip clean water from the end of the brush on to the paint to make it spread and form a marbled pattern covering the whole triangle. Repeat for the other triangle and leave to dry.

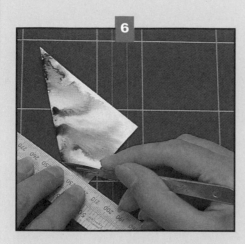

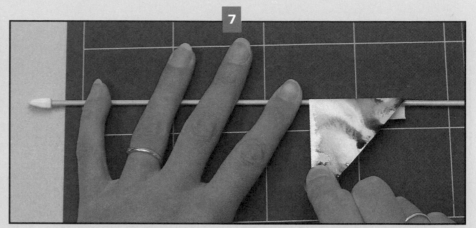

6 Measure the length of the silver coil. Starting at corner C, mark this length off along edge CA on one of the triangles and cut off any excess straight across the top.

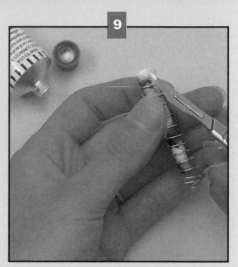

7 To help the paper triangle to curl more easily, lay it face down, then lay a knitting needle across it (parallel with line CA); while pressing on the knitting needle, grasp a corner of the paper and pull it round the needle. Repeat two or three times until the paper begins to curl up.

8 Roll the paper round the knitting needle to form a tube. Repeat steps 6-8 with the other triangle.

9 Insert a paper tube into a silver coil, leaving corner B out, and allow it to expand to fill the coil. Glue corner B down, then remove the tube from the coil and give it a light coat of matt varnish. Repeat for the other tube. Leave the tubes

to dry slotted on to the knitting needle. When dry, push the tubes back into the coils.

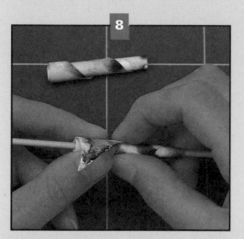

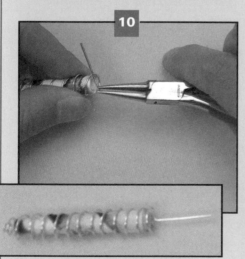

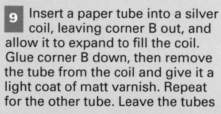

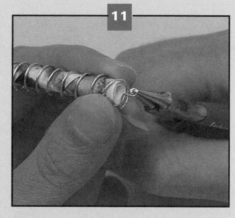

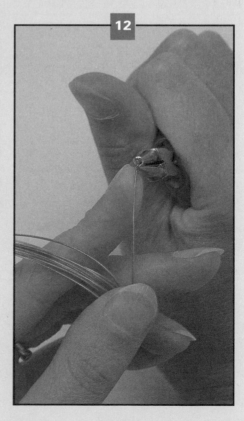

11 Cut off the end of the wire to leave a 7mm (¼in) length and form the end into a loop.

10 With the pliers, bend the remaining end of silver wire at an angle of 90° as shown, so that it crosses the end of the paper tube and holds it in place. Halfway across the end of the tube, bend the wire again at a 90° angle (see inset) so that it stands vertically.

12 To make the earring attachments, form a loop on the end of the 0.7mm (¹⁄₃₂in) wire. To centre the loop on the wire, loosen the grip on the pliers, slide them round to the other side of the loop, grip gently and push back the wire where it joins the loop.

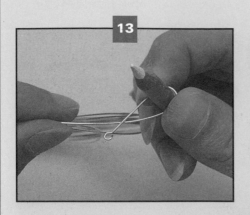

13 About 20mm (¾in) along from the loop, wrap the wire over the pencil and double it back to form a 'U' shape. Snip the wire, leaving the end 2-3mm (⅛in) shorter than the end with the loop.

14 Insert the cut end of the wire between the wide end of the pliers and bend back slightly. The inset shows how the finished earring attachment should look.

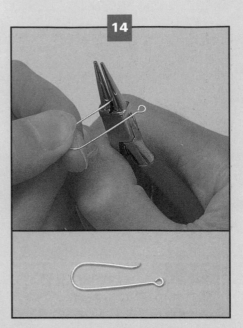

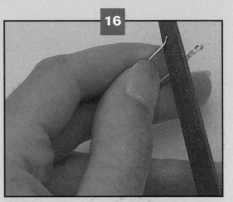

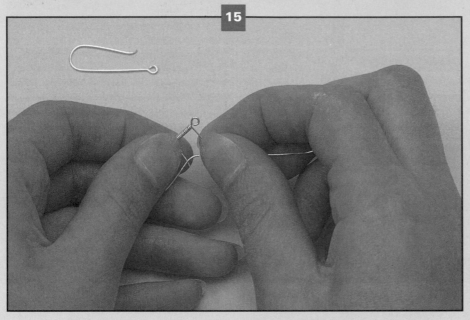

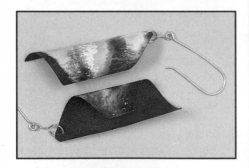

ALTERNATIVE DESIGN

Using similar paper rolling techniques, different shaped earrings can be achieved by changing the shape of the card and rolling methods. We show you an alternative here, created using an equilateral triangle which is rolled asymmetrically (along the dotted line shown).

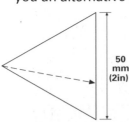

50 mm (2in)

15 Cut a 10cm (4in) length of 0.4mm (¹⁄₆₄in) silver wire and wrap it tightly round the ear wire, starting just above the loop, for 7mm (¼in). Snip off the ends and squeeze them on to the ear wire.

16 File the end of the ear wire by gently rubbing it on the ring file. This is to take the sharpness off the edge of the metal — do not file to a point. Open up the loop on the end of the silver coil (made in step 11), slip the loop of the ear wire into it, then close up the loop again.

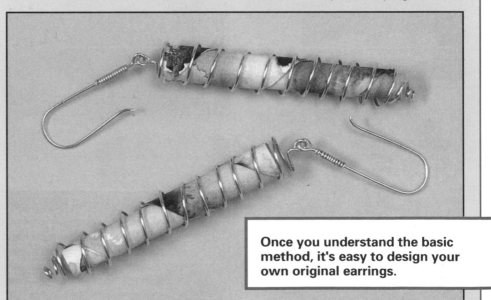

Once you understand the basic method, it's easy to design your own original earrings.

PAPERCRAFT

PIERCED LAMPSHADE

In this project we introduce you to the art of ornamental pierced paper work and use the technique to make a parchment lampshade decorated with nursery motifs.

MATERIALS

To make the lamp shown *below left* you will need:

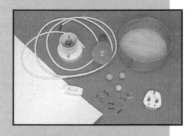

Above, imitation parchment paper at least 400 x 480mm (16 x 19in); round box of thin plywood, 144mm (5¾in) diameter and 75mm (3in) deep (from craft shops); 2m (2yd) electrical flex; on/off switch; electric plug; 40-watt light bulb; electric screw-on light fitting with screws and nuts to fit; 3 screws 16mm (⅝in); 3 small wood balls (from hardware shops); 7 'poppa' eyelets.

Above, tracing paper at least 40 x 48cm (16 x 19in); stiff white paper, 40 x 48cm (16 x 19in); small leather off-cut; hard fibre board approx 20 x 38cm (8 x 15in); newsprint; masking tape.

Above, long metal ruler; scalpel; small pair of scissors; reaming awl; screwdriver; bradawl; small hammer; 5mm (³⁄₁₆in) round file; eyelet assembling tool; 2 paper clips; HB pencil; H pencil; eraser; cutting board.

This lampshade is very simple to make, yet when the lamp is switched on at night the effect is magical, with tiny pin pricks of light forming a delicate tracery against the soft glow of the paper.

Paper has traditionally been used for making lampshades, the Japanese spherical shade made of paper stretched over a frame of bamboo being the best known example. However, it can be more inventive and effective to let the paper create its own structure without needing the support of a frame. Our lampshade is simply a cylinder of stiff paper riveted together in a decorative way at the join and supported by a plywood base.

To make an attractive shade, choose a handmade paper, which has more character and texture than machine-made paper. We have used an imitation parchment paper which casts a warm, mottled, creamy glow when the light is behind it, as well as being quite sturdy when assembled. When choosing a sheet of paper, always hold it up to the light so that you can judge its effect when used as a lampshade.

Piercing the paper

The figurative design on our lampshade is punched into the paper using a reaming awl, a punching tool that produces larger holes than the more traditional pin or needle. This has the effect of letting a little more light through and therefore defining the pattern better.

When designing your own shade, try to incorporate the seam into the design. Here it has been cut into a scalloped edge to echo the scalloped seam on the box base.

TEMPLATE

48cm
(19in)

1 Use the bradawl to make a small hole in the base of the plywood box, then use the small round file to enlarge the hole enough to push the electrical flex through.

2 Thread the flex through the hole and connect it to the light fitting. Centre the light fitting on the base, then push the point of the file through the screw holes to mark their positions on the base.

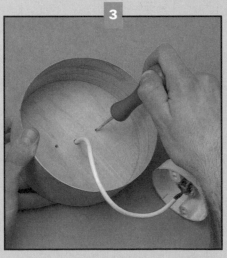

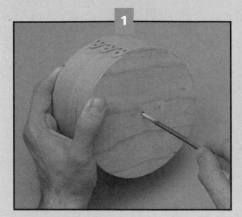

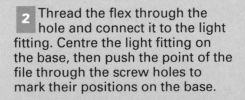

3 Pull the light fitting to one side and use the bradawl to make the holes for the screws that will secure the light fitting to the base.

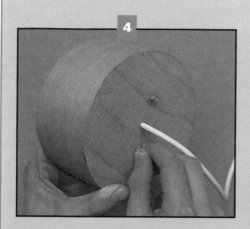

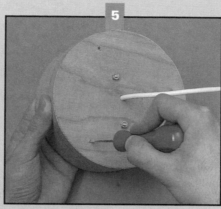

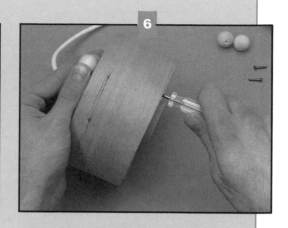

4 Re-position the light fitting and screw it to the base. Secure the screws with their matching nuts on the underside of the box and tighten securely.

5 Make three equidistant pencil marks 15mm (⅝in) in from the edge of the underside of the box. This is to mark the positions of the wooden ball feet. Punch small holes with the bradawl.

6 Make a small hole in each of the wooden balls with the bradawl and screw them in position on the underside of the box. Cut the electrical flex in half and fit the on/off switch. Fit the electric plug to the other end of the flex.

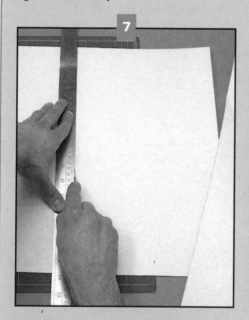

7 Use a scalpel and steel ruler to cut out a rectangle 40 x 48cm (15¾ x 19in) from the parchment paper. Ensure that each of the corners is a perfect right angle.

8 Enlarge the template (in sections) on a photocopier at 200%, then again at 135%. Join up the sections. Lay tracing paper over the template and trace over the lines with an HB pencil, including the scalloped edges. Turn the tracing paper over and go over the lines again with the HB pencil (do not rub the back of the sheet with pencil as you would normally).

Turn the tracing paper right way up again and tape it to the parchment paper. Go over the pattern lines once again, this time with an H pencil, in order to transfer the pattern to the parchment paper.

HELPFUL HINT

When doing pierced paper work, it is best to punch through a sheet of stiff paper laid over a thick, soft surface such as a wad of newsprint or an old blanket. The stiff paper offers a slight resistance, making neater holes, and the soft surface gives you something to push into with the awl; also the edges of the holes are pushed through to the inside and create a soft effect.

9 Remove the tracing. Tape the parchment paper to a sheet of stiff white paper, then lay this on a thick wad of newsprint. Go over all the pencil outlines with the reaming awl, piercing a series of small, evenly spaced dots about 4mm (⅛in) apart. Pierce the scalloped edge on the left but not the one on the right.

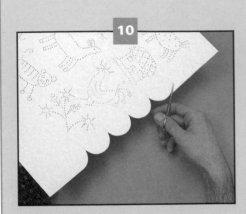

10 Remove all the pencil marks around the holes with a clean eraser. Cut along the scalloped edge on the right with small scissors.

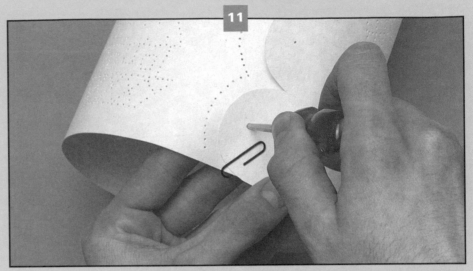

11 Roll the paper to form a cylinder, with the scalloped edge overlapping the straight edge. Secure at both ends with paper clips. Check that the cylinder fits snugly into the wooden base; make it larger or smaller if necessary and secure again with the paper clips. Using the reaming awl, pierce the holes marked on the centre of each scallop, piercing through both layers of paper. Push the eyelets in place.

12 Lay the cylinder, scalloped edge down, on the hard fibre board covered with a piece of leather to protect the paper. Working inside the cylinder, place the eyelet assembling tool over the eyelet and tap it in place with a hammer. Repeat for all the eyelets.

13 Carefully slide the completed lampshade into the wooden box.

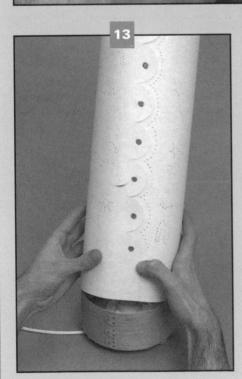

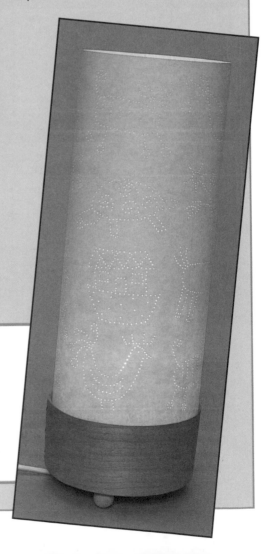

Pierced decoration is a folk craft found in many cultures — at festival time in Mexico you still see examples of cut and pierced tissue paper decorations, while in North Africa tin lanterns are pierced to give an eerie, magical effect.

SURFACE DECORATION

DECORATED MOUNT

MATERIALS

To make the line and wash picture mount shown *below left* you will need:

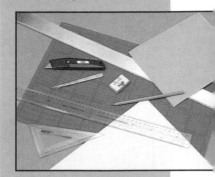

Above, sheet of mounting board 76 x 102cm (30 x 40in); sharp craft knife; scalpel; metal straight edge; perspex ruler; set square; cutting mat; HB pencil; eraser; sheet of fine grade sandpaper.

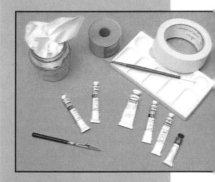

Above, watercolour paints: burnt umber, alizarin crimson, viridian, ivory black, Chinese white; gold gouache paint; ruling pen; palette; watercolour paintbrush, round size 4; water jar; tissues; masking tape; gummed brown paper tape.

The right mount and frame can enhance the visual impact of any painting, print or drawing. In this project we show you how to make a bevelled picture mount decorated in the traditional way with lines and washes.

A mount is a flat piece of board or card with a window cut in the centre through which the picture is visible. Its function is to focus attention on the image by by creating a 'breathing space' between it and the frame. The width and colour of the mount has a strong influence on the overall look of the picture, so it is important to make a careful choice.

Most watercolour and pastel paintings benefit from a fairly wide mount and a narrow frame, since this enhances the airiness and delicacy of the work. However, this will depend very much on the size of your painting; generally the smaller the picture the wider the mount should be. The only 'rule' is that the mount margin at the bottom of the image should be wider than at the top and sides otherwise, due to an optical illusion, the bottom will appear smaller than the other margins.

The colour of the mount should be chosen carefully to complement the image and not overpower it. Our traditional costume print, for example, has a light cream mount which picks out the background of the picture, enhancing the delicacy of the image.

Cutting the mount

Most mounts have a bevelled edge: the edges of the window slope down towards the picture. This gives a more pleasing look than abrupt right-angled cuts, and also eliminates unwanted shadows on the image. You will need a metal straight edge (a heavy steel ruler with a bevelled edge) to guide the knife blade when cutting out the window. The blade must be razor sharp so that you can cut cleanly with a single pass of the knife. Practise on scrap pieces of mounting board before cutting your mount.

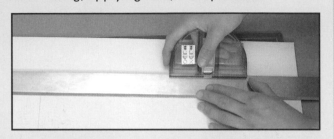

USING A MOUNT CUTTER

If you intend mounting several pictures it may be worth investing in a mount cutter, which automatically cuts the bevelled edge of the mount at an angle. When using a mount cutter, hold the metal straight edge firmly and cut along its straight edge — not the bevelled edge. Starting about 2mm (1/16 in) in from the corners, dig the blade into the mounting board and draw the cutter along, applying firm, even pressure.

1 Measure the width and height of your picture and decide on the width of the borders (the side and top borders should be of equal width, and the bottom border should be slightly deeper). From these measurements you can calculate the size of board to cut from the sheet of mounting board (our picture area measures 305 x 215mm (12 x 8½ in); the top and side borders measure 70mm (2¾ in) and the bottom border measures 85mm (3⅜ in); the size of the board you need is therefore 460 x 355mm (18⅛ x 14in)). Cut the board accurately against the straight side of the metal straight edge. Mark the position of the window opening with a pencil, and rule the lines, overlapping them at the corners. Check the right angles with a set square.

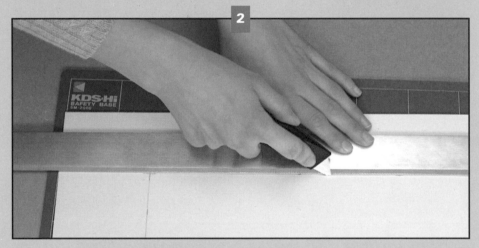

2 Using the tip of the scalpel blade, make a small hole at each corner of the window opening. Lay the metal straight edge along one of the pencil lines, with the bevelled edge facing inwards. With a craft knife, cut along the line at a constant angle of 50-60°. Repeat for the other three sides of the window. Smooth any jagged edges with fine sandpaper.

3 Lightly draw the guidelines for the wash and the lines using a pencil and perspex ruler: starting 5mm (3/16 in) from the window opening, draw two lines 5mm (3/16 in) apart, then leave a gap of 10mm (3/8 in) and draw two more lines 5mm apart. Use a set square to check that the corners are perfect right-angles.

LINES AND WASHES

Our mount is given a period touch by the addition of lines and washes. As with the mount itself, choose colours that complement those in the picture. Before applying the broad colour washes, dampen the area between the ruled lines with a soft brush dipped in water. The colour will then flow more evenly on to the paper.

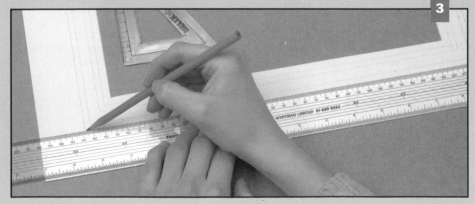

USING A RULING PEN

The best way to achieve perfectly straight lines is to use a ruling pen. This has an adjustable screw on the side of the nib, allowing you to alter the thickness of the line. To fill the pen, load a brush

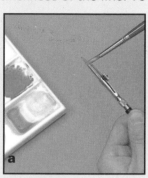

with ink or paint and transfer it to the reservoir of the nib, **a**. Draw the line against a bevelled ruler placed upside down so that the bevel creates a small gap, preventing the ink or paint from touching the ruler directly and so avoiding the risk of smudging, **b**.

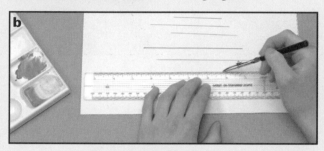

4 Dilute viridian watercolour paint to a very pale tint. With a soft brush, dampen the wash band with clean water, making sure you don't go over the pencil lines. When this is almost dry, paint the band very carefully, holding the brush at a low angle with the tip held against the pencil line. Leave to dry.

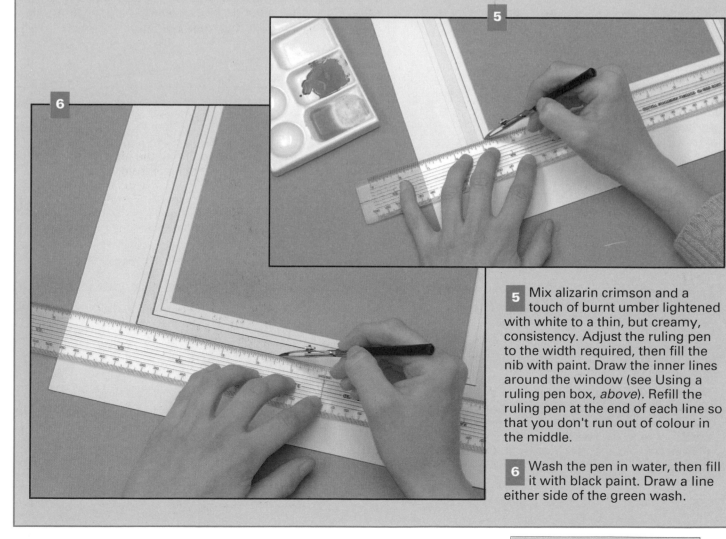

5 Mix alizarin crimson and a touch of burnt umber lightened with white to a thin, but creamy, consistency. Adjust the ruling pen to the width required, then fill the nib with paint. Draw the inner lines around the window (see Using a ruling pen box, *above*). Refill the ruling pen at the end of each line so that you don't run out of colour in the middle.

6 Wash the pen in water, then fill it with black paint. Draw a line either side of the green wash.

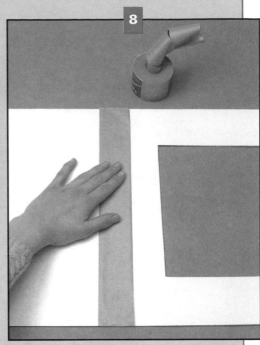

7 Wash the ruling pen again, then open it a fraction (by adjusting the screw) and draw a slightly wider line using gold gouache paint. Leave to dry.

8 Cut out the backing board to the same dimensions as the mount. Turn the window mount upside down and place it with its top edge butted up against the edge of the second piece of board. Join the two pieces with gummed brown paper tape.

9 Secure the top of the picture to the backing board with masking tape. Close down the window mount, check that the picture is correctly positioned, then tape the bottom edge to the backing board.

The decorative possibilities of line-and-wash mounts are endless. You can vary the number and width of lines and the space between them, and you can choose whether to use one colour or several. Next time you visit an art gallery take note of the frames and mounts of the pictures — they will give you plenty of ideas to experiment with.

PRINTMAKING

MONOPRINT WITH STENCILS

A monoprint is a way of creating a unique one-off print. In this project you can experiment using the technique of monoprinting with stencils to create an attractive image with all the qualities of line, texture and colour of a relief print.

In this monoprinting project a series of hand-cut paper stencils are secured to a glass sheet by a clear printing medium. Shapes are cut out and lifted away, creating a stencil which is subsequently inked up and printed. This process is repeated with freshly cut stencils so that selected areas are cut out and printed to build up the image as a progressive process. The drawing is finally added on top of the stencilled colours by using a tracing process. The process is quite complex, so read through the step-by-step instructions before you begin each stage.

Japanese wood-block printers of the 17th and 18th centuries made use of stencils to apply colour to wood-blocks. Paper shapes would be cut to the design on the master block, and each shape for a particular colour would be inked up individually. The shapes would then be assembled on the block and printed. The final design was then inked up in black and printed on top of the colours.

At the turn of the 20th century the French painter Edgar Degas turned monoprinting into a serious art form. He produced a definitive series of black and white monoprints which have proved to be some of his most powerful graphic work. Swiss artist Paul Klee devised a technique of inking paper with colour to use as coloured carbon paper. He used this to apply coloured line designs on top of watercolours and drawings, to give a monoprinted result.

War shortages
The monoprinting technique was taken up by artists during the Second World War, when many printmaking studios were closed, and printmaking materials were in short supply. Monoprints could be easily produced by artists in their own studio or home, using just glass or metal plates.

Each monoprint is a unique piece of work, and part of its appeal is that it cannot be repeated to reproduce an exact copy.

MATERIALS

To make the stencilled monoprint shown *below left* you will need:

Above, sheet of glass 415 x 585 x 3mm (16½ x 23 x ⅛ in); six sheets of crystal parchment 730 x 980mm (28¾ x 38½ in), halved; black waterproof felt-tip pen; 2 sheets of cartridge paper 415 x 585mm (16½ x 23in); masking tape; tissue paper; scalpel; newsprint.

Above, Japanese baren 100 x 100mm (4 x 4in); small inking roller; oil-relief printing ink colours: vermilion, orange, cobalt, olive green, black; tube of reducing medium; 5B pencil; white spirit; palette knife; rag; card off-cut; sheet of glass 305 x 250mm (12 x 10in) for inking.

HELPFUL HINT

If you wish to alter the colours of ink suggested for the fish monoprint, choose sharply contrasting colours so that your monoprint has dramatic impact. To test out a different colour scheme, make a quick colour sketch using felt tip pens, or using acrylic paint.

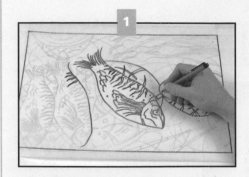

1 With the 5B pencil draw up the design on a sheet of cartridge paper. Place a sheet of crystal parchment on top of the design and use masking tape to secure it around the edges. With the black felt tip pen trace the design on to the crystal parchment.

2 Cover the work surface with a sheet of newsprint. Place the glass sheet on the newsprint. Turn over the design and position it centrally, face down, on the glass sheet. Secure with masking tape.

3 Turn over the glass sheet and place it down on the newsprint again (the design will now be under the glass sheet). Place a sheet of cartridge paper on the glass sheet to cover the design. Use a strip of masking tape to fix its top edge to the glass. Fold it back to reveal the design.

4 Squeeze a small quantity of reducing medium on to the small glass sheet. Use the roller to spread it out evenly. Take the roller and spread a thin coating on to the large glass sheet, covering the design and allowing for a slight overlap all round. Take a sheet of crystal parchment and place it on to the rolled area, pressing down gently and evenly so that the paper sticks to the glass. Clean the small glass sheet using a rag and white spirit.

THE DESIGN

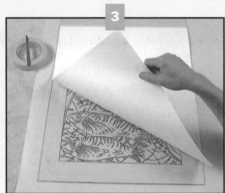

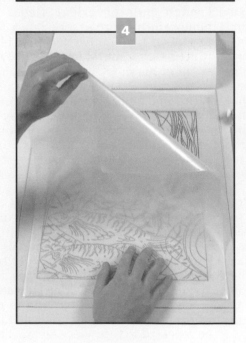

5 With the scalpel, cut round the outlines of all the fish. Cut out the shadows underneath the two bowls, leaving the top of the chopsticks intact. Carefully lift out all the cut-out pieces of the stencil, using the scalpel blade, and discard.

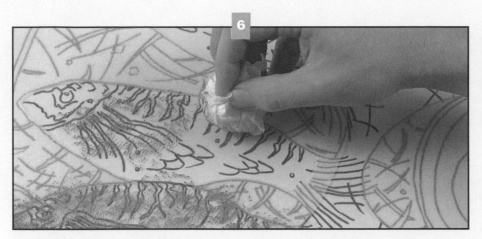

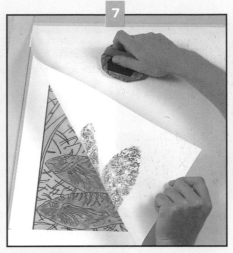

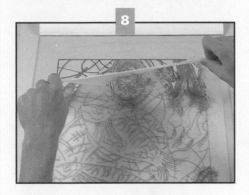

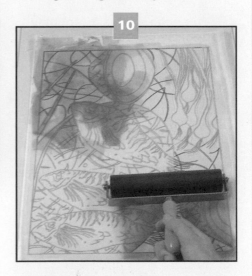

6 Squeeze a small quantity of orange printing ink on to the small glass sheet. Add a touch of vermilion red and mix with the palette knife. Crumple a piece of tissue paper into a small ball and press into the ink. Dab the tissue paper lightly on to the glass in the exposed areas of the stencil, creating a mottled effect. Repeat the dabbing until all the exposed areas are well covered.

7 Remove the film of crystal parchment and discard from the glass. Mask off the edges of the design with the cartridge paper cut-offs. Carefully bring the sheet of folded-back cartridge over so that it covers the inked surface of the glass. Use the Japanese baren to smooth over the paper, pressing gently. Lift the paper once or twice to check that the impression is coming through evenly all over.

8 Use the rag and white spirit to thoroughly clean off both glass sheets. Remove the masking strips from the edges of the design and place on one side. Repeat step 4 (rolling out the reducing medium and covering the glass with crystal parchment). Use the scalpel to cut round and remove the shape of the chopsticks, the inside of the tea bowls and the green stems of the onions.

Crumple some tissue paper to make two small balls. Squeeze out a small quantity of orange ink on to the small glass sheet and use one paper ball to dab on to the chop sticks. Squeeze out some olive green and dab with the second paper ball on to the remaining cut-out areas. Use both hands to remove and discard the crystal parchment.

Replace the masking strips around the design. Fold over the cartridge paper and print, rubbing with the baren as before. Clean the glass sheets thoroughly. Remove the masking strips and set aside.

9 Repeat step 4 (rolling out the reducing medium and placing the crystal parchment on the glass). Use the scalpel to cut out and remove the shape of the plate and bowls. Squeeze a small quantity of red ink on to the small glass sheet and, taking the card cut-off, dip the edge into the paint. Press it repeatedly on to the exposed areas of glass, reloading the card frequently with paint. Fold the card in half and continue pressing the V-shaped edge on to the glass until an irregular criss-cross pattern is obtained. Remove the parchment, replace the masking strips, fold over the cartridge paper and smooth with the baren to print as before. Clean the glass sheets thoroughly.

10 Repeat step 4. Use the scalpel to cut out and remove the shaded areas: the end of the chopsticks, the fish tails and below the bowls. Spread the reducing medium on the small glass sheet, adding a touch of cobalt to produce a transparent blue colour. Use the roller to apply the colour to the cut-out areas, taking care not to tear the parchment. If the stencil starts to lift, press down gently. Remove the parchment, replace the masking strips, fold over the cartridge paper and use the baren to print as before. Clean the glass sheets.

11 Repeat step 4 (rolling out the reducing medium and placing the crystal parchment on the glass). Use the scalpel to cut out and remove the background area and the inside of the plate (not the shadowed areas or the spring onions). Squeeze out some black ink on to the small sheet of glass and use the roller to spread it over the crystal parchment. Use the illustration of the finished monoprint as reference and, with the 5B pencil, trace some fine curving pencil lines through the ink to produce a patterned effect on the plate and tablecloth. Remove the crystal parchment and discard, replace the masking strips, fold over the cartridge paper and use the baren to print as before.

12 Take off the masking strips. Remove the masking tape and lift the printed cartridge paper carefully from the glass. Leave to dry. In the sun this could take two hours — indoors, it should be left overnight. Clean the glass sheets thoroughly.

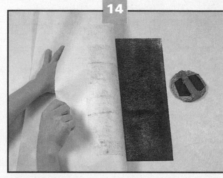

13 When the print is thoroughly dry, use the scalpel to cut a piece of cartridge paper to exactly the same size. Place the large glass sheet on the work surface and the cartridge paper on the glass sheet. Squeeze out some black ink on to the small glass sheet and use the roller lightly, both vertically and horizontally, to spread it to a thin film on the cartridge paper. Make the covering quite dense but not solid black.

14 Remove the paper from the glass and lay it on the newsprint on the work surface. Place a sheet of newsprint over the inked surface and use the baren to rub over the newsprint so that excess ink is absorbed.

15 Remove the design from the back of the large glass sheet and position the right way up on the dry print. Secure with masking tape along one edge to stop it moving. Lift and fold it back while the inked sheet of cartridge is

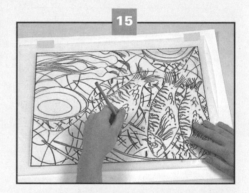

placed face down directly on top of the print. Replace the design on top of the inked cartridge paper. Using the 5B pencil, trace over the lines of the design so that they appear in black on the coloured print.

16 Check that the outline is coming through evenly by lifting up the design and the inked cartridge paper at intervals. When the design is completed leave to dry. As the ink is very lightly applied drying time will be relatively short.

For first-time printmakers this method of printing is ideal as it requires very little specialist equipment. It also minimises the mess! By using sheets of glass for rolling out the inks and discarding the cut stencils immediately after printing there is much less chance of spills or splashes.

PAPERCRAFT

ZOETROPE

In this papercraft project we show you how to construct a zoetrope, an amusing optical adult toy that was popular in the first part of the 19th century because it demonstrated an early form of animation. We also introduce you to the fascinating history of the development of the moving image.

The zoetrope was one of a number of adult optical toys developed in the early part of the 19th century to exploit the newly discovered phenomenon of the persistence of vision.

Anyone who has ever watched a firework display has experienced the phenomenon of persistence of vision — the fact that the brain retains an image for a brief interval after the eye sees it, so that fireworks appear to leave a trail of light in the sky. It was a phenomenon that caught the imagination of the exploratory minds of the 19th century — and it led from the early optical toys to, eventually, the development of the moving cinematic image and, ultimately, to television.

Spinning disc
The earliest — and simplest — of the optical toys was the thaumatrope, which consisted basically of a card disc with threads either side for holding it. The disc bore two related images (such as a horse and carriage, or St George and a dragon), one on each face, and when the disc was spun by twisting and untwisting the threads, the two images were seen as one picture.

Early animation
The zoetrope was a more sophisticated toy. It consisted of a revolving cylinder with vertical slots in it, into which was placed a strip of paper with figures or other images in different stages of movement. When you looked through the slots while the cylinder was revolving, you seemed to see a moving picture. In our zoetrope you will see a flickering black-and-white animated figure with hat and cane, resminiscent of the early movies. When making your own designs you will find that two-tone — and especially black-and-white — images are particularly dramatic when animated in your zoetrope.

MATERIALS

To make the zoetrope shown *below left* you will need:

Above, foam board 78 x 52cm (30 x 20in); 300gsm (140lb) A1 (33⅛ x 23⅜in) white paper; jar lid; 300gsm (140lb) A1 (33⅛ x 23⅜in) black paper; 4cm (1⅝in) of 25mm (1in) dowel; 5cm (2in) of 6mm (¼in) dowel; 6.5mm (¼in) washer; 1.5mm (¹⁄₁₆in) nail, 12mm (½in) long.

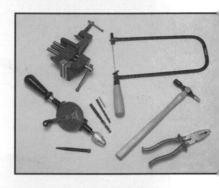

Above, hand drill and 1mm (¹⁄₃₂in), 5mm (³⁄₁₆in) and 7mm bits (¼in); vice; fretsaw and fine blade; hammer; centre punch; pliers.

Above, cutting mat; sandpaper grade 120; sanding block; carbon paper; steel ruler; compasses; scissors; craft knife; small block of wood; black felt-tipped pen; HB pencil; all-purpose glue; epoxy resin glue; black spray paint; white acrylic paint; medium-sized hog's hair paintbrush; mixing palette.

STENCILS

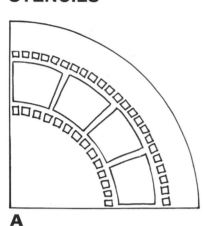

A

B

C

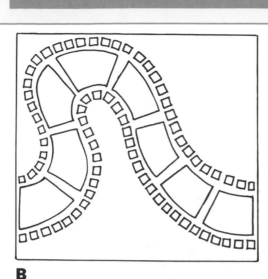

1

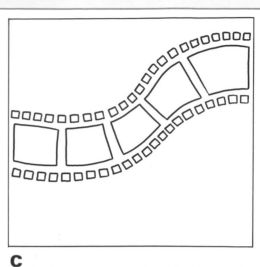

1 To make the base of the zoetrope, set the compasses to 10cm (4in) wide and draw a circle 20cm (8in) in diameter on the sheet of foam board, then draw an inner circle 5cm (2in) in diameter, using the same centre point. Cut out the large circle using a fretsaw and fine blade. Smooth the edge of the circle with sandpaper wrapped around a sanding block.

2

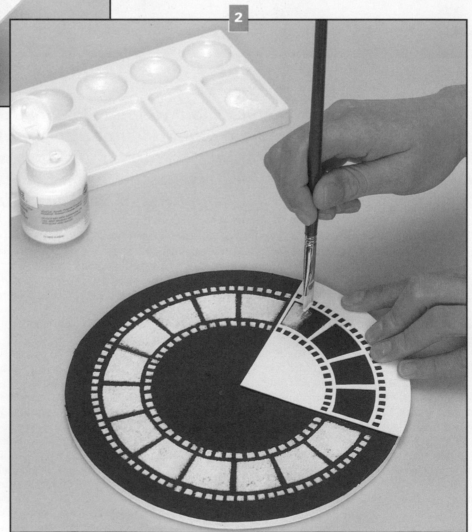

2 On the sheet of black paper draw another circle 20cm (8in) in diameter, cut it out and glue it to the top of the foam board circle (the top being the side without the inner circle drawn on it). Enlarge stencil A on a photocopier to 200%. Trace the stencil on to the sheet of white paper. Using a scalpel, cut around the outline and carefully cut out the 'reel of film' pattern. Place the stencil with the corner at the centre of the black circle and stipple undiluted white acrylic paint through the holes using a hog's hair paintbrush. Turn the stencil through 90° and repeat until the circular pattern is complete.

diagram 1 (all measurements in mm: 25mm = 1in)

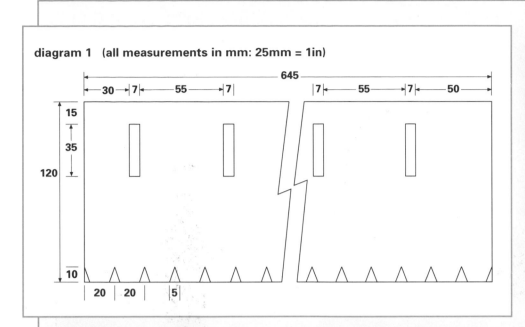

3 To make the outer wall of the zoetrope, mark out the dimensions on the black paper as shown in diagram **1**. Cut out the windows and the V-shaped tabs using the craft knife and ruler.

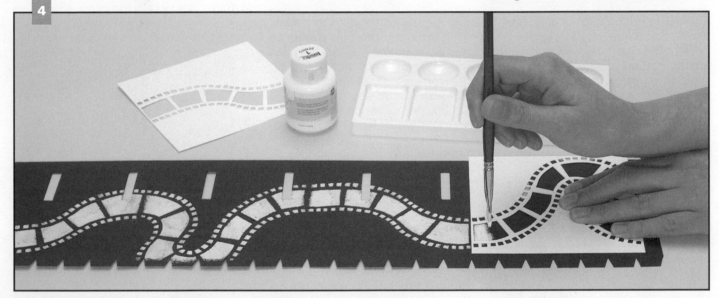

4 To make the 'reel of film' pattern on the outer wall, enlarge stencils B and C to 200%, then trace them on to the white paper and cut them out. Pour some white acrylic paint on to the mixing

palette. Lay the outer wall flat on the work surface, with the V-shaped tabs nearest to you. Starting at the left end, hold stencil B in place on the wall, butted up to the left and upper edges, and stipple white

paint through the holes. Use stencil C next, and carry on stencilling in this way, following diagram **2**, reversing the stencils as necessary.

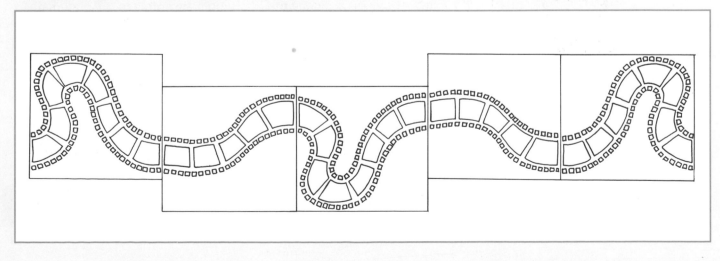

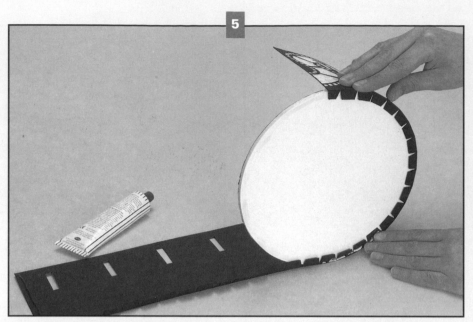

5

6

5 Using the craft knife and steel ruler, score a line along the back of the outer wall, where the V-shaped indents come to a point. Bend the tabs inwards along the scored line. Apply glue to the insides of the tabs and along one of the overlapping edges of the wall, then wrap the wall around the base as shown, pressing the tabs firmly in place. Glue the overlapping edges together, ensuring that the pattern joins up neatly where the edges overlap. Leave to dry.

6 Set the compasses to 2.5cm (1in) and draw two circles on the foam board. Cut out the circles with a fretsaw and fine blade, then glue one on top of the other. Smooth off the edges using sandpaper wrapped around a sanding block. Rest the circle on a small block of wood and drill a hole through the centre using a hand drill and 5mm (³⁄₁₆in) drill bit.

7 With a fretsaw, cut a 5cm (2in) length of 6mm (¼in) dowel and clamp it upright in the vice. Using the hand drill and 1mm (¹⁄₃₂in) bit, drill a hole about 5mm (¼in) deep into the end of the dowel. Shape the end to a point using sandpaper. With pliers, clip off the head of the 1.5mm (¹⁄₁₆in) nail, leaving it 10mm (³⁄₈in) long. Apply glue to the cut end of the nail and insert it into the hole, leaving 5mm (³⁄₁₆in) of the tip protruding from the dowel.

7

8

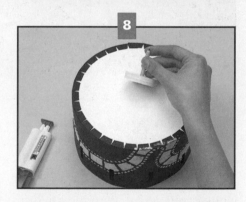

8 Apply epoxy resin glue to the other end of the dowel and push it firmly into the hole in the circle made in step 6. Glue the whole assembly to the underside of the zoetrope base, placing it on the 5cm (2in) diameter circle originally drawn on the base.

diagram 3

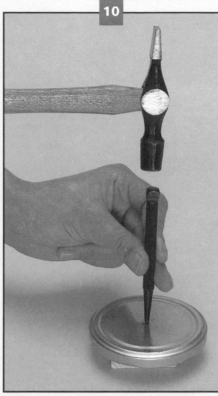

10 Use a centre punch and small hammer to make a dent (not a hole) in the centre of the jam jar lid, resting the lid on a small block of wood for support.

9 Use the fretsaw to cut a 4cm (1⅝in) length of 25mm (1in) dowel. Clamp it upright in the jaws of the vice and use a 7mm (¼in) bit to drill a hole in the centre, drilling right through to the other end.

11 Glue a washer (inside diameter 6.5mm (¼in) to one end of the piece of 25mm (1in) dowel. Using epoxy resin glue, glue the other end of the dowel to the centre of the jam jar lid, first roughening the area to be covered by the dowel with sandpaper to give the surface a 'key'.

12 Spray the support and the underside of the base of the zoetrope with black paint. To avoid spraying the sides with paint, hold the aerosol can directly above the zoetrope and place a piece of scrap card near the edge to catch any stray paint droplets.

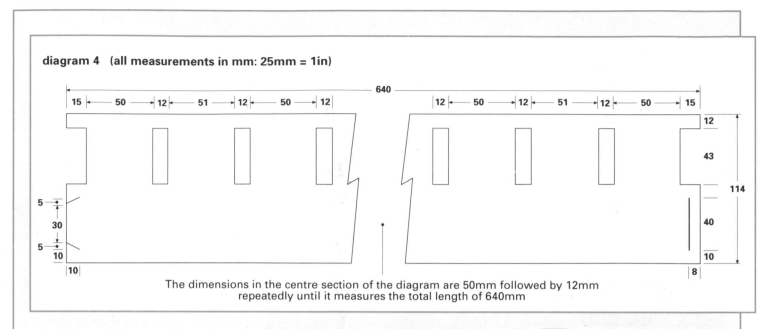

diagram 4 (all measurements in mm: 25mm = 1in)

640

15 — 50 — 12 — 51 — 12 — 50 — 12 | 12 — 50 — 12 — 51 — 12 — 50 — 15

12

43

114

5
30
5
10

40

10

10

8

The dimensions in the centre section of the diagram are 50mm followed by 12mm repeatedly until it measures the total length of 640mm

13 Mark out the dimensions of the inner wall as shown in diagram **4** on the white paper. Cut out the inner wall using the craft knife and steel ruler, and cut out the windows. Lightly mark the centre point between the windows in pencil. Enlarge the figures in diagram **3** to 160% and trace them on to the inner wall, placing them centrally between the windows and about 2mm (1/16in) up from the bottom edge. Fill in the shapes with black felt-tipped pen.

14 When the black spray paint is completely dry, slot the zoetrope into the hole in the support. Gently bend the inner wall round and slot the tab on the right edge into the vertical cut on the left edge. Hold in place with a paper clip and slide the inner wall inside the outer wall, making sure the two sets of windows line up with each other.

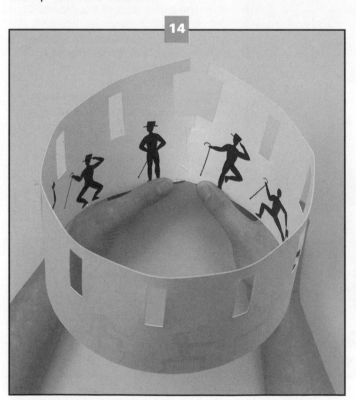

Because the inner wall of the zoetrope is removable, you can create as many designs as you like — and it gives you a wonderful opportunity to experiment with animation.

SHADOW PUPPET

Shadow puppets, one of the most ancient forms of puppet, create magical effects when operated behind an illuminated translucent screen. In this project we show you how to make a shadow puppet based on traditional designs.

Shadow puppets are thought to have originated in India or China. In India they were traditionally used to depict stories from the Hindu epics — the *Mahabharata* and the *Ramayana* — and there is a theory that these puppets developed from the characters depicted on the painted boards that travelling storytellers used to relate these stories.

Shadow puppets have developed as a strong tradition in other parts of the world, and in Indonesia religious epics are also enacted through shadow puppetry, although in a different style. Here the puppets are accompanied by a gamelan (percussion) orchestra, and one puppeteer or 'dalang' brings the puppets to life. Originally dalangs were priests, and shows would revolve around religious rituals, and the summoning up of gods and spirits to pray for good harvests. Women were only allowed to watch the shadows, but the men were also permitted to watch from behind — a rule that no longer applies.

Puppet characters

Shadow puppets are treated with respect and have great symbolism. In Java the noble characters always have pointed noses and look downwards (being humble). They are often blue or dark coloured. Arrogant or evil characters, such as demons or devils, have round noses, are often red and look upwards. Traditionally the characters are always kept apart from one another when packed away, and when a puppet reaches

the end of its working life it is ceremonially floated down a river.

Shadow puppets are generally considered to be the easiest type of puppet to construct. They can be opaque or translucent, and were traditionally made from leather; modern puppets, however, are often made from other materials. Our shadow puppet is made from ivory board, a thin card that is treated with vegetable oil to give it translucency. It is a character inspired by the court jester of Western culture, but designed with an Eastern influence in its movement and construction, and in its face, which can be interpreted as sideways or forward-looking.

MATERIALS

To make the shadow puppet shown *below left* you will need:

Above, A3 (16½ x 11¹¹/₁₆in) sheet of ivory board; black waterproof Indian ink; waterproof drawing inks: scarlet, sunshine yellow, bright green; 2 long green plant sticks; black bead thread (or button thread, doubled); sewing needle; scrap of acetate (or plastic packaging material); vegetable oil; handwriting carbon paper; paper towels.

Above, scissors; pencil; paintbrushes, fine and medium; paper hole punch; eraser; junior hacksaw; craft knife; hammer; newsprint; scrap of wood; leather hole punches (or anvils and wad punch adaptor), 1mm (³/₆₄in), 2mm (⁵/₆₄in) and 3mm (⅛in).

Above, cardboard box, 57 x 12.5 x 79cm (22 x 5 x 31in); craft knife; metal straight edge; double-sided matt draughting film, 50 x 65cm (20 x 26); scissors; masking tape; pencil; G-clamp; lamp.

1 Enlarge the templates on a photocopier at 200% and trace them lightly on to the sheet of ivory board using carbon paper. You will need to trace the pieces for the legs, arms and hand twice. Do not transfer the marks for the punched holes, they are for guidance later.

2 Cut the pieces out roughly and, using a fine paintbrush and black Indian ink, go over all the lines except the pupils of the eyes.

TEMPLATES

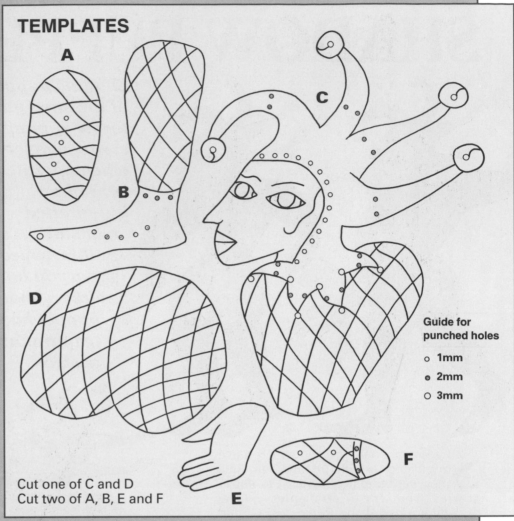

A

B

C

D

E

F

Guide for punched holes

○ 1mm
● 2mm
○ 3mm

Cut one of C and D
Cut two of A, B, E and F

3 Carefully cut round the outside edge of the outlines with scissors.

4 Hold the pieces up to the light against a window pane (or use a light box), and trace the lines through to the other side of the pieces with pencil. Go over the pencil lines with ink using the small brush, and also paint the edges of the pieces (holding them away from the work surface as shown).

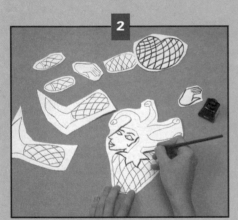

HELPFUL HINT

Although the ink dries quickly, be careful not to smudge it. If you make a mistake when you are painting, scratch the mark off with a sharp scalpel. Don't try to cover it with white paint or correction fluid as this will show later when the oil makes the paper translucent. Wash the brush in soapy water between colours.

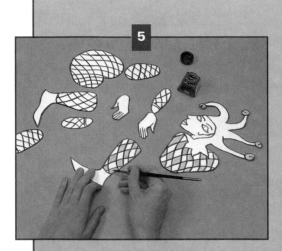

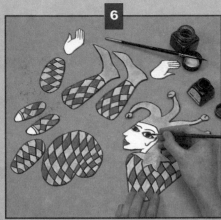

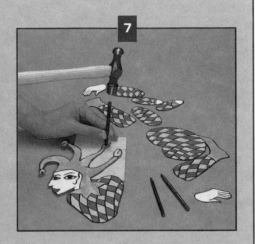

5 Start painting the pieces with the medium-sized paintbrush. Paint yellow ink on alternate diamonds and on the bells of the jester's cap, then paint a yellow line underneath each eye. Paint the corresponding areas on the reverse side of the puppet (hold the pieces up to the light to help you locate the same areas).

6 Paint the remaining diamonds, the lips and a line above each eye with scarlet ink. Paint the reverse side as in step 5. Paint the cap, feet and cuffs on both sides with green ink. With the small brush and black ink, paint both sides of the pupils (traditionally the eyes are painted last, as this is thought to give the puppet its soul).

7 With the leather punches and a hammer, and working on a small piece of wood or vinyl-covered cork tile, make holes in the pieces (see box *below*) using the template as a punching guide.

PUNCHES

Strike the punch sharply with the hammer, slightly lifting the punch to counteract the hammer blow. This action takes some practice, but it will prolong the life of your punch. We have made the holes with leather punches as used by shadow puppet makers in India. You can buy similar punches in the form of holders with interchangeable attachments ('wad punch adaptors' and 'anvils') from specialist craft shops and mail order suppliers.

8 Cover the table with newsprint and apply vegetable oil generously to both sides of all the pieces with paper kitchen roll. Rub it in until the oil saturates the card so that it becomes transparent. Wipe off any excess oil with clean kitchen roll. You can leave the oil to soak in overnight if you wish, or continue to work on newsprint or plastic to protect the work surface.

9 Punch out small discs of acetate using a paper hole punch. These will be used as washers to strengthen the joins.

JOINING THE PIECES

The torso should overlap the lower half of the body. One arm should be arranged with the pieces on top of the torso, the other arm with the pieces behind the torso. The legs should be arranged in the opposite way. This will prevent the limbs from catching on each other when the puppet is operated. The pieces should be joined about 5mm (¼in) away from the edges.

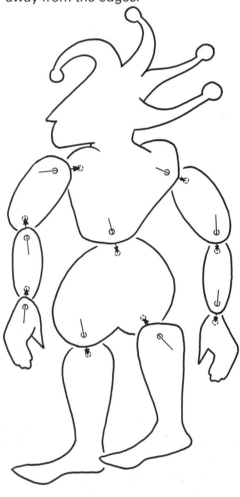

10 Lay out the pieces in the order in which they will be joined (see box *right*). Start by joining the two main pieces of the body. Thread a sewing needle with bead thread and knot the thread at the end. Put one of the acetate discs on the eraser and pierce the centre of the disc with the needle.

11 Push the acetate disc on to the needle and thread and push the needle through the two body parts from the front as shown. Use the eraser as a 'thimble' to help you push the needle through if necessary. Pull the thread tight.

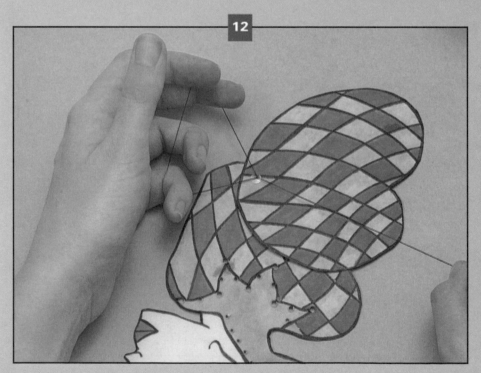

12 Push the needle through another acetate disc and start making a simple knot, but before pulling the loop tight hold it open with two fingers as shown, then with the thumb of the same hand press on the disc while you pull the knot tight with the other hand. Tie a second knot and cut the thread. Join the legs to the body, then join the upper arms, lower arms and hands, using the diagram *above* as reference.

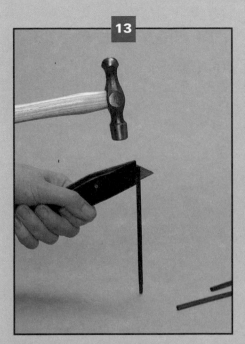

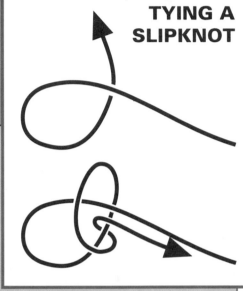

TYING A SLIPKNOT

13 With the hacksaw, cut two 23cm (9in) lengths of plant stick. Cut another piece 13cm (5in) long and split it in half with a craft knife and hammer as shown.

14 On the side of one of the 23cm (9in) plant sticks, cut a notch 5mm (¼in) from one end. Thread the needle with a length of bead thread, tie a simple knot at the other end, then tie a slipknot (see diagram *right*). Slip the loop of the knot over the end of the stick and into the notch. Pull to tighten. Pierce an acetate disc as in step 10 and push it on to the thread.

15 Take the needle through one of the puppet's hands as shown, then thread another acetate disc on to the needle and thread.

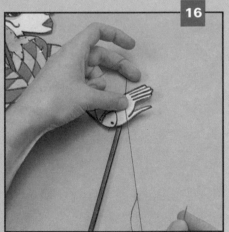

16 Leaving enough thread to enable the stick to be held at right angles to the puppet and have some mobility, turn the puppet over and tie two or three knots on the other side as in step 12. Attach the other 23cm (9in) stick to the other hand, repeating steps 14-16.

17 Cut notches on the curved sides of the split 13cm (5in) sticks 1cm (⅜in) from either end and in the middle. Sandwich the head of the puppet between the flat sides. Thread the needle, tie a knot in the end of the thread and take the needle through the puppet next to the top notch. Take the thread through the corresponding notch on the back of the puppet and push the needle back through to the front. Pull the thread across the front notch and knot it securely to the other end of the thread. Trim the ends. Repeat for the other

17

MAKING A SCREEN

Take a shallow cardboard box and secure any weak joins or corners with tape. If you are using a box the same size as ours, cut a 42 x 58cm (16 x 23in) window in the front for the screen. Cut off the back of the box and most of one end. Stick the draughting film to the inside of the window with masking tape as shown *below*.

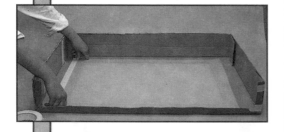

OPERATING THE PUPPET

Secure the box to the edge of a table with a G-clamp and fix a lamp in position so that it shines from above on to the back of the screen. The lamp we have used has a fluorescent tube, but an anglepoise lamp works just as well. Ideally the screen should be at a slight angle, leaning away from the puppeteer.

Hold the puppet flat against the screen and manipulate it as shown *below*. Hold the puppet in a definite pose so that the audience has long enough to interpret the meaning of the gesture before the puppet is moved into a different position.

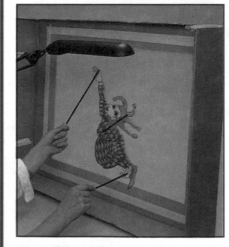

We have made a very basic screen to show off our shadow puppet, but you could construct a more substantial one from wood, or adapt a light box.

PAPERCRAFT

MAGIC FOLDER

MATERIALS

To make the magic folder shown *below left* you will need:

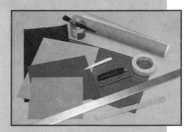

Above, sheet of 1mm (¹⁄₃₂ in) greyboard, 400mm x 200mm (16 x 8in); piece of black bookcloth, 60mm x 160mm (2½ x 6¼in); primed linen canvas off-cut, 250mm x 280mm (10 x 11in); A4 (11¾ x 8¼in) sheet of thick red paper; craft knife; masking tape; bone folder; fine grade sandpaper; PVA (white) glue; cutting mat; steel rule; metal ruler; pencil; 20mm (¾in) decorator's brush.

Above, newsprint; sheet of A5 (8¼ x 5⅞in) card; thin strip of card, 10mm x 70mm (⅜ x 2¾in); 2 wooden boards, A4 (11¾ x 8¼in) size; acrylic paint, sap green or permanent green; acrylic retarder; saucer or palette; metallic gold powder; approximately 6 fresh oak leaves; small soft paintbrush; 12mm (½in) decorator's brush.

Our 'magic' folder puts to use some of the bookbinding techniques you have learned in previous projects, and the inside of the folder is printed with a design of oak leaves in red and gold, using acrylic paint and metallic gold powder.

Our intriguing and attractive folder is a variation on the magician's stock-in-trade, the 'magic wallet' used in the 'disappearing bank note' trick. These wallets have three identical folding sections, but when the wallet is opened and closed only two sections can be seen at a time. The bank note is inserted into one section of the open wallet and the magician closes it. Then, using sleight of hand, he re-opens the wallet on the opposite side, revealing two empty sections: the bank note appears to have vanished.

Our folder is slightly different in that it has only two folding sections and the bank note, instead of vanishing completely, appears to move from one side of the folder to the other by itself. The secret lies in the construction of the folder and the arrangement of the two sets of black strips on the inside.

For the cover of the folder we have used artist's primed linen canvas; the 'reverse' side has an attractive texture and is hard-wearing, while the primed side, being non-porous, will not shrink or distort when glued to the folder.

How it works

Open the folder and slip a bank note under the strips, either on the left or the right. Close the folder, then distract the attention of your audience with some theatrical hand waving and abracadabras while you slyly manouvre the folder so that when you open it again, hey presto! the bank note has magically jumped from one side of the folder to the other.

1 Take the sheet of greyboard and gently bend it in both directions to find the grain direction (see Stationery Box). Mark the grain direction with an arrow. Using a craft knife and steel rule, cut four pieces of greyboard measuring 160mm x 90mm (6⁵⁄₁₆ x 3½in), with the long measurement following the direction of the grain.

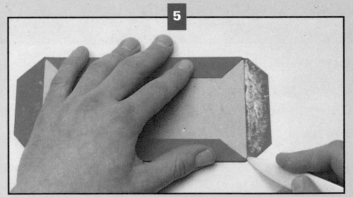

2 With a sheet of fine sandpaper, gently smooth and round off all the sharp edges and corners of the boards. This will make it easier to wrap the canvas and paper around the boards later on and help give a more professional finish.

3 Cut two 130mm x 200mm (5⅛ x 7⅞in) pieces of canvas and two pieces of red paper the same size (with the long measurement in the direction of the paper grain). Lay a sheet of newsprint on the work surface, then place one of the cut pieces of paper on it and stipple it with PVA (white) glue using the 20mm (¾in) decorator's brush.

4 Discard the newsprint and position one of the cut boards centrally on the glued sheet of paper with an even margin of 20mm (¾in) all the way round. Press the board firmly to the paper. With a craft knife, cut all four corners of the red paper at 45°, positioning the cuts 3mm (⅛in) from the corners of the greyboard.

5 Fold the long edges of the paper over on to the board and press in place, rubbing with the bone folder to smooth out any wrinkles. With the sharp end of the bone folder, tuck in the corners of the paper on both short edges, then fold over the flaps and press down on to the board, again using the bone folder to smooth out any bumps.

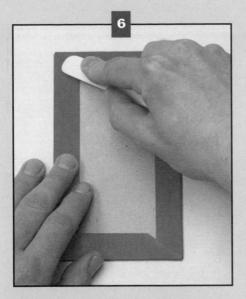

6 The corners where the flaps meet must be absolutely flat, so rub firmly over these areas with the bone folder to give a smooth finish. Repeat this process of gluing and pressing for the remaining piece of red paper and the two pieces of canvas. When all four pieces of board are glued up, place them back-to-back, sandwiched between sheets of newsprint, and press them between the two wooden boards with a heavy weight placed on top. Leave to dry for at least an hour.

7 Remove the boards from the press and place one of the red boards on a sheet of newsprint. Squeeze out about 4cm (2in) of green acrylic paint on to the mixing palette and mix to a smooth consistency with a few drops of acrylic retarder. Using the small paintbrush, quickly paint the veined sides of the leaves.

HELPFUL HINT

Acrylic paints dry very quickly, so if you wish to keep the paint workable for longer you should mix it with acrylic retarder, a translucent gel that slows the rate of drying.

8 Arrange the leaves paint side down on one of the red boards. Cover with a sheet of newsprint and then the A5 (8¼ x 5⅞in) sheet of card. Press firmly and evenly with your hand to leave the leaf impression on the red board.

9 Remove the card, newsprint and leaves from the red board. Using a small strip of card, sprinkle the gold powder evenly over the painted impression. The gold will stick to the paint where it is dusted, with a few green areas showing through. Leave to dry for at least an hour. Repeat the painting and printing process for the second red board.

10 Cut two lengths of black bookcloth 30mm x 150mm (1³⁄₁₆ x 5⅞in). Glue the reverse sides and press them together to make one strip. Leave to dry for 20 minutes. Using a craft knife and steel rule, cut the strip lengthways to make 4 lengths 6mm x 150mm (¼ x 5⅞in).

11 Dust the excess gold powder off the painted boards with a clean dry brush. Protect the painted side of both boards with newsprint, securing it to the back of the boards with masking tape.

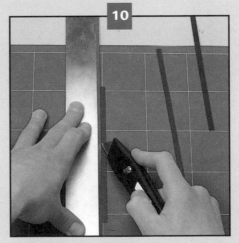

12

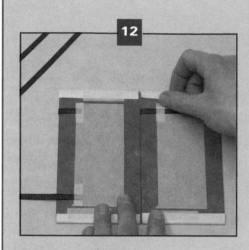

12 Place the boards on the work surface, butted up to each other and painted side down. Make a pencil mark 25mm (1in) from the top and bottom lefthand edges of both boards (labelled A and B in the Lacing diagram, *right*). Line up one of the black strips with the pencil mark on the top left of board A so that it overlaps the board by 30mm (1³⁄₁₆in). Secure the end to the board with masking tape. Feed the strip around the other side of the board, pull tightly and secure to board B, as shown. Repeat with a second black strip, lined up with the pencil mark at the bottom left of board A.

LACING DIAGRAM (all measurements in mm: 25mm = 1in)

A BACK   B BACK

25   40
1   4   1   3
2   3   4   2
25   40
30   30   30   30

13

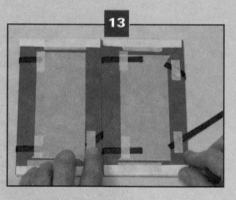

13 Make a pencil mark 40mm (1⅝in) from the top and bottom right edge of both boards. Secure the remaining two black strips to board B, this time at a 45° angle (see diagram). Feed the two lengths around the other side of board B so they criss-cross, and pull tight before securing the overlaps to board A.

14 Place the boards on a fresh sheet of newsprint and remove the masking tape securing the sheets protecting the painted side of the boards. Stipple PVA (white) glue on to the backs of the red boards and the canvas-covered boards and press them together back-to-back. Leaving the protective sheets of newsprint in place on the painted faces of the folder, close it and place it between the pressing boards. Place a heavy weight on top and leave to dry overnight.

14

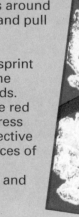

The printing technique used here could be effectively employed for making greetings cards. The combination of paint and gold powder gives a luxurious, slightly embossed effect that is not possible with gold paint, as the latter dries to a dull finish. Metallic powders are available in copper, silver and lemon yellow as well as gold.

PAPERCRAFT

PAPER CHAMELEON

MATERIALS

To make the paper chameleon shown *below left* you will need:

Above, sheet of 3.2mm (⅛in) foam board, 52 x 64cm (21 x 25in); 2 sheets of 380gsm (185lb) card, 52 x 64cm (21 x 25in); sheet of 1.5mm (¹⁄₁₆in) white card, 53 x 81cm (21 x 32in); cutting mat.

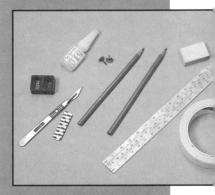

Above, H and HB pencils; pencil sharpener; eraser; steel ruler; scalpel and spare blade; removable transparent tape; tube of powerful adhesive such as Superglue; 2 round-headed drawing pins.

The fascination of paper sculpture is that something dynamic and three-dimensional can be created out of a flat piece of paper or card. In this project we show you how to make a paper chameleon, which is ingeniously designed to balance on the edge of a desk or bookshelf.

In previous papercraft projects we have introduced the basic techniques of cutting, scoring, folding and glueing paper, and in this project we bring all these skills together to make a splendid paper sculpture of a chameleon.

Geometric constructions

Essentially, paper sculpture relies on the basic constructional forms of the cube, pyramid, cone and cylinder. Some of these forms, and variations on them, have been used to make the main body of the chameleon, and detailed templates for these are given overleaf. Although the sculpture looks quite complex, it is very easy to assemble. However, it is a good idea to make up each of the sections 'dry', to check that everything fits before glueing it together. Also, you might find it helpful to label the

back of each template lightly in pencil as there are quite a few of them!

To achieve the optimum effect, the white paper and card must appear as clean and crisp as possible, so it is important to keep your work space, tools and hands clean while working. Clean your ruler by rubbing it along a sheet of paper folded over the edge of a table. You should also try to handle the model as little as possible during its construction. Because the structure is fairly heavy when complete, for greater strength it is advisable to use a good-quality brand of Superglue, rather than ordinary glue, when assembling it. Alternatively you could use double-sided tape; this is clean, quick and simple to use, and if you need to take anything apart the bond can be released by applying solvent or lighter fluid to a loosened edge.

137

TEMPLATES

HEAD
photocopy the template
at 159%

TONGUE
photocopy the template
at 100%

TAIL
photocopy the template
at 100%

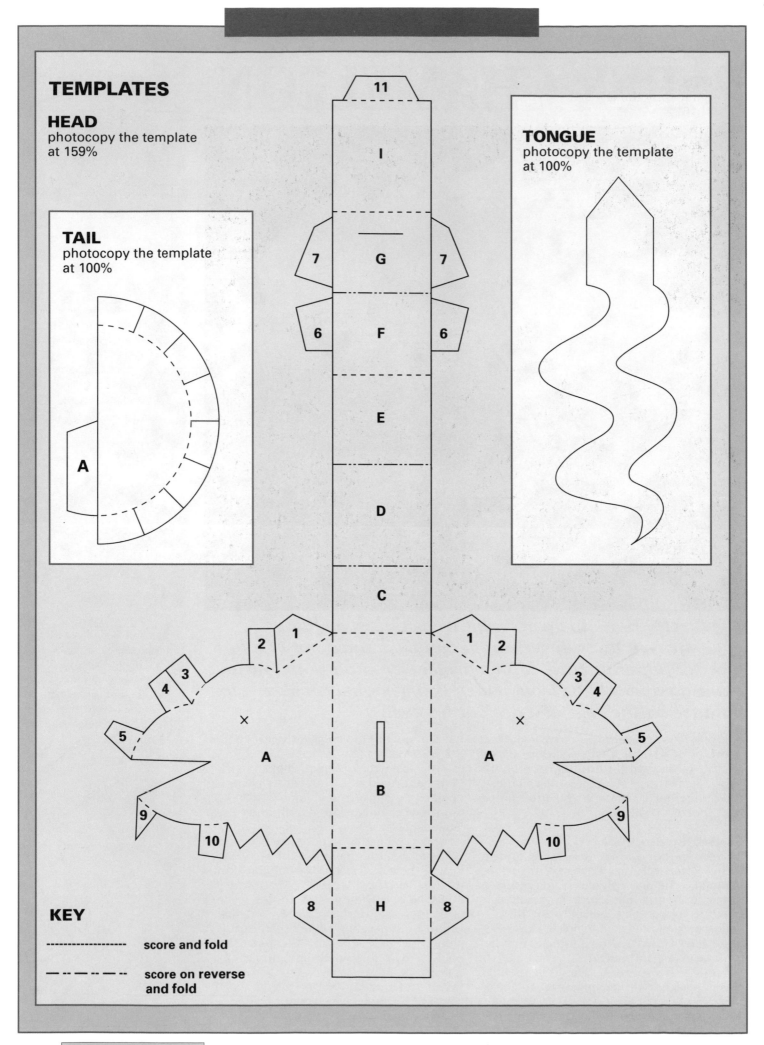

KEY

- - - - - - - - - - - **score and fold**

- · - · - · - **score on reverse and fold**

BODY
photocopy the template
at 168%

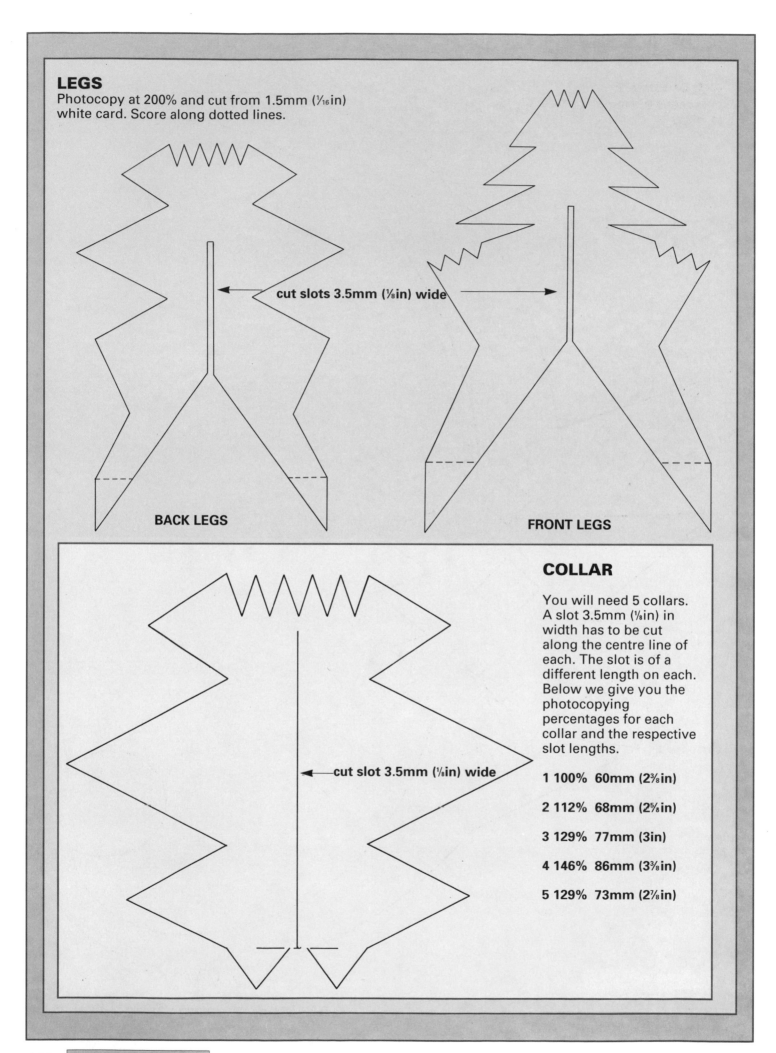

LEGS

Photocopy at 200% and cut from 1.5mm (¹⁄₁₆in) white card. Score along dotted lines.

cut slots 3.5mm (⅛in) wide

BACK LEGS

FRONT LEGS

COLLAR

You will need 5 collars. A slot 3.5mm (⅛in) in width has to be cut along the centre line of each. The slot is of a different length on each. Below we give you the photocopying percentages for each collar and the respective slot lengths.

1 100% 60mm (2⅜in)

2 112% 68mm (2⅝in)

3 129% 77mm (3in)

4 146% 86mm (3⅜in)

5 129% 73mm (2⅞in)

cut slot 3.5mm (⅛in) wide

VERTEBRAE

Line ab: position and length of slot TOP **Line de: position and length of slot** TOP

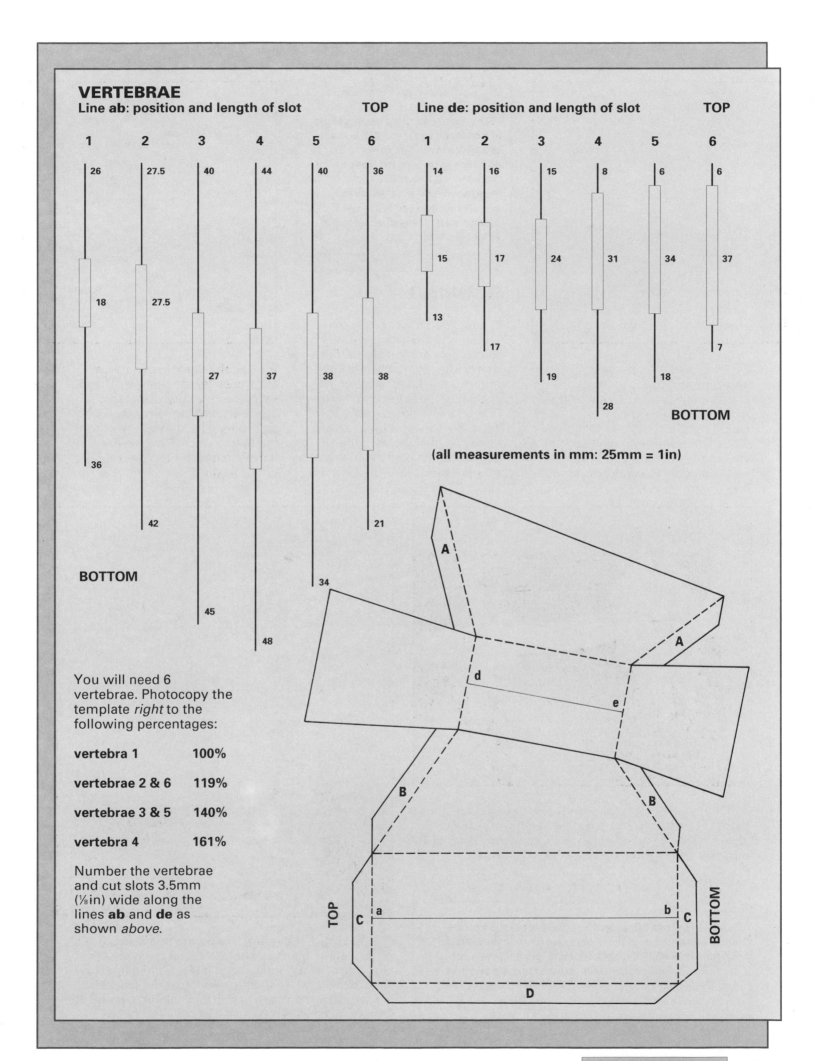

1	2	3	4	5	6
26	27.5	40	44	40	36
18	27.5	27	37	38	38
36	42	45	48	34	21

BOTTOM

1	2	3	4	5	6
14	16	15	8	6	6
15	17	24	31	34	37
13	17	19	28	18	7

BOTTOM

(all measurements in mm: 25mm = 1in)

You will need 6 vertebrae. Photocopy the template *right* to the following percentages:

vertebra 1 100%

vertebrae 2 & 6 119%

vertebrae 3 & 5 140%

vertebra 4 161%

Number the vertebrae and cut slots 3.5mm (⅛in) wide along the lines **ab** and **de** as shown *above*.

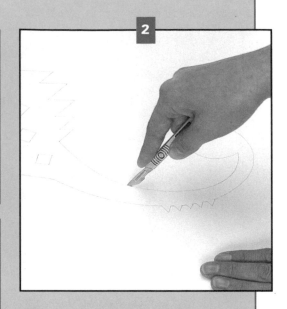

SCORING

When using thick card and paper, scoring makes it easier to produce accurate folds. Put a metal ruler along the fold line and run the 'blunt' edge of the scalpel blade along it to mark a line on the surface of the paper. To make curved scores, make a series of small holes in the surface of the paper with the point of the scalpel blade.

1 Enlarge the templates according to the instructions on each template. Turn each sheet over and rub over the lines (including the score and fold lines) with a soft pencil (you will see the lines more clearly if you hold the sheet up against a window pane).

2 Lay the spine template on the sheet of foam board and secure with transparent tape. Trace around the template with an H pencil to transfer the lines to the foam board. Remove the template and cut out the shape with a scalpel.

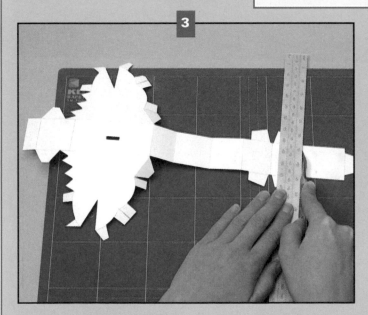

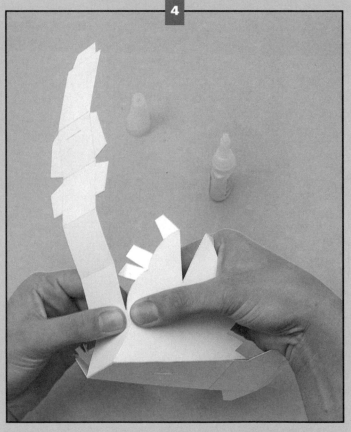

3 On the sheets of 380gsm (185lb) paper, trace and cut out the templates for the head, vertebrae, collars, tongue and tail detail. Cut, score and fold each template where indicated (see Scoring, *above*).

4 To construct the head, bend the two face pieces A at right angles to panel B. Fold in the two sets of tabs 1 and 2 and apply a spot of Superglue to each. Press panel C on to the tabs and hold in place for a few seconds. Continue in this way, gluing panel D to tabs 3 and panel E to tabs 4 and 5.

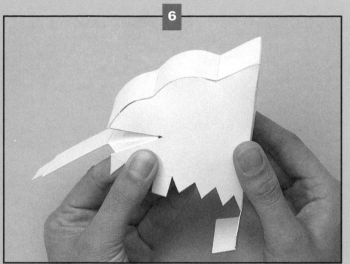

5 Fold panel F to fit along the upper line of the mouth, then glue tabs 6 and slide them inside the head as shown. Press the tabs in place inside the head.

6 Line up the edges of panel G with the edges of the lower part of the mouth. Glue up tabs 7 and slide them into place on the inside of the head.

7 Holding the head upside down, glue up tabs 8. Fold panel H in as shown and gently press it down so that, viewed from the side, it is hidden by the 'fringes' at the base of the face panels A.

8 Bend tabs 9 and 10 inwards and dab a spot of glue on each. Glue the end of panel H, then fold panel I over and push tab 11 into the slot in panel H, pressing along the glued edge to secure the panel firmly in place.

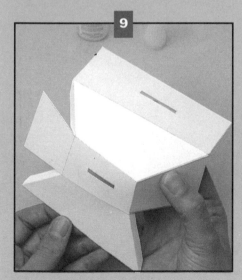

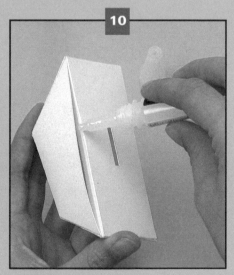

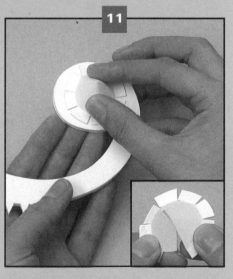

9 Now start making up the vertebrae pieces. Fold in the tabs marked A, B and C on the template, glue them up and fold the panels along the fold lines to form a 'box'.

10 Squeezing the ends of the 'box', push tab D into the remaining opening and glue it up to complete the 'box'. Repeat for the remaining five vertebrae.

11 Now make the tail detail. Score and fold where indicated on the template, then glue up tab A and bring the two ends together to form a cone (see inset). Glue on to the end of the tail as shown.

12 The chameleon is now ready to be assembled. Starting with vertebra number 6, slot each vertebra on to the front section of the body (see Helpful Hint, *below*).

HELPFUL HINT

Push the vertebrae on to the body with care as the barbed shape at the end is a weak point and could tear if too much pressure is applied. Hold the barb with finger and thumb while you push the first slot in the vertebrae on until the end of the barb comes through the other slot. Then grasp the end of the barb and gently pull the vertebrae along on to the body.

13 When all the vertebrae are in place, push the head on to the barb and gently push down so that it 'clicks' into place. Push the tongue into the slot in the mouth, then push the drawings pins for the eyes in place either side of the head.

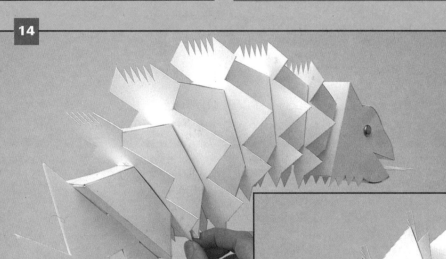

14 Place the collars in position between the vertebrae, following the size order given in the templates. Collar number 1 goes between the first and second vertebrae. The best method is to hold the chameleon by the spine, push the collar down as far as it will go without forcing it, then pull it through from underneath.

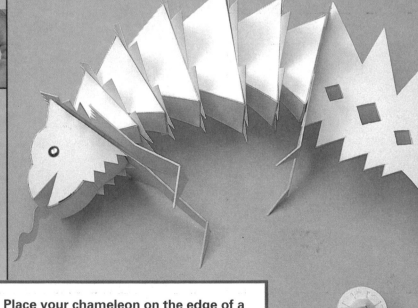

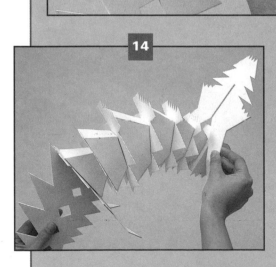

15 Finally, push the leg pieces into place behind the head and in front of the tail. Make sure both sets of feet are facing forwards.

Place your chameleon on the edge of a desk or bookshelf, with back and front feet resting on the surface, and it will balance there quite happily. If you wish, you could decorate your chameleon with paint or paper collage.